THE MASTER PLAN

ALSO BY MICHAEL HEALEY

1979
Courageous
The Drawer Boy
Generous
The Innocent Eye Test
Kicked
The Nuttalls
Plan B
Proud
Rune Arlidge

with Kate Lynch:
The Road to Hell

adaptations:
The Physicists (Friedrich Dürrenmatt)
On The Rocks (George Bernard Shaw)
Olympia (Ferenc Molnár)
The Front Page (Ben Hecht and Charles MacArthur)

THE MASTER PLAN

MICHAEL HEALEY

Based on *Sideways: The City Google Couldn't Buy* by Josh O'Kane

PLAYWRIGHTS CANADA PRESS
TORONTO

First edition: September 2023
Printed and bound in Canada by Imprimerie Gauvin, Gatineau

Jacket art and design provided courtesy of Crow's Theatre
Author photo © Graham Isador

Playwrights Canada Press
202-269 Richmond St. W., Toronto, ON M5V 1X1
416.703.0013 | info@playwrightscanada.com | www.playwrightscanada.com

LIBRARY AND ARCHIVES CANADA CATALOGUING IN PUBLICATION
Title: The master plan / Michael Healey.
Names: Healey, Michael, 1963- author.
Description: A play.
Identifiers: Canadiana (print) 20230494323 | Canadiana (ebook) 2023049434X
| ISBN 9780369104809 (softcover) | ISBN 9780369104823 (EPUB)
| ISBN 9780369104816 (PDF)
Classification: LCC PS8565.E14 M37 2023 | DDC C812/.54—dc23

Playwrights Canada Press operates on land which is the current and ancestral home of the Anishinaabe Nations (Ojibwe / Chippewa, Odawa, Potawatomi, Algonquin, Saulteaux, Nipissing, and Mississauga), the Wendat, and the members of the Haudenosaunee Confederacy (Mohawk, Oneida, Onondaga, Cayuga, Seneca, and Tuscarora), as well as Metis and Inuit peoples. It always was and always will be Indigenous land.

We acknowledge the financial support of the Canada Council for the Arts, the Ontario Arts Council (OAC), Ontario Creates, and the Government of Canada for our publishing activities.

Canada Council for the Arts | Conseil des arts du Canada
ONTARIO ARTS COUNCIL
CONSEIL DES ARTS DE L'ONTARIO
an Ontario government agency
un organisme du gouvernement de l'Ontario
ONTARIO CREATES | ONTARIO CRÉATIF
Canada
Ontario

This is for Morwyn,
without whom it would all be pointless.

The Master Plan was commissioned and first produced by Crow's Theatre, Toronto, from September 5 to October 1, 2023, with the following cast and creative team:

Christopher Allen: Cam Malagaam, Designer, Sidewalk Labs
Ben Carlson: Will Fleissig, CEO, Waterfront Toronto
Philippa Domville: Meg Davis, Chief Development Officer, Waterfront Toronto
Peter Fernandes: Tree, a Norway maple residing at 134 Yorkminster Road
Tara Nicodemo: Kristina Verner, Vice President, Strategic Policy and Innovation, Waterfront Toronto
Yanna McIntosh: Helen Burstyn, Board Chair, Waterfront Toronto
Mike Shara: Dan Doctoroff, CEO, Sidewalk Labs

Chris Abraham: Director
Joshua Quinlan: Set and Props Designer
Ming Wong: Costume Designer
Kimberly Purtell: Lighting Designer
Thomas Ryder Payne: Sound Designer
Amelia Scott: Video Designer
Jennifer Parr: Stage Manager
Maya Bowers: Assistant Stage Manager

CHARACTERS

Kristina Verner: Vice President, Strategic Policy and Innovation, Waterfront Toronto
Meg Davis: Chief Development Officer, Waterfront Toronto
Dan Doctoroff: CEO, Sidewalk Labs
Cam Malagaam: Designer, Sidewalk Labs, Toronto office
Tree: Norway maple, residing at 134 Yorkminster Road
Will Fleissig: CEO, Waterfront Toronto

Helen Burstyn: Board Chair, Waterfront Toronto
John Tory: Mayor, City of Toronto
Steve Diamond: Waterfront Toronto board member
Micah Lasher: Communications, Sidewalk Labs
Eric Schmidt: Executive Chairman, Alphabet Inc.

Justin Trudeau
Kathleen Wynne
Siemens
Quayside Edge Joint Venture
Speaker Nunziata
Councillor Jaye Robinson
Urban Forestry Staff
David Stonehouse
Michael Williams
Matthew Pegg
Julie Di Lorenzo
Doug Ford
Saadia Muzaffar
John Ruffolo
Chair, Privacy and Ethics Committee

Peter Kent
Josh O'Kane
Sundar Pichai
Silent Lawyer
Silent Consultant
Voices

NOTES

{These brackets indicate a timeline animation.}
[These brackets indicate a video or photo projection.]
Italicized dialogue in scene one indicates direct address.

Everyone in the city-building game looks fantastic. Even the shabbily dressed are chic. Glasses and accessories are breathtaking. Tree wears a snazzy track suit.

Locations are suggested.

PRESHOW

As the audience enters the theatre, they are confronted with a projection on a scrim or monitor: an enormous head, disembodied and floating gently. The head of CHRIS *Abraham.*

[The head gazes at the patrons and says, randomly, "hello," "welcome," "welcome back," and "we were promised a flying car."]

The lights go down. The head addresses the now-seated audience:

CHRIS: We were promised a flying car. Instead, we got this:

[A blooping noise, and the head suddenly has green, pointy goblin ears.]

[Through the following the head changes ears, acquires a variety of human and animal noses, hats, facial hair, and finally becomes fully animated.]

Good evening or good afternoon. I'm Chris Abraham, Artistic Director of Crow's Theatre. As you know, an event of theatre is a collaboration between artists and an audience. As artists in rehearsal, we are constantly speculating on how an audience will receive our work. We wonder what you need, what the most effective ways are to tell you our story. To be blunt: until you show up, we're guessing.

And now you're here, and we are eager to find out what you think of our work. In the past, we've had to rely on how loud your applause was at the end of the play to assess how we did. The thing is, applause is a lousy way to quantify artistic success. It's unspecific. It's . . . untrustworthy.

But now we are in a position to analyze what each audience member is experiencing in real time. Each of your seats is equipped with a sensor, and it records each time your posterior shifts (which might indicate restlessness or boredom). It can also measure increased blood flow to an audience member's midbody region, which could indicate a state of arousal.

We have also placed extremely sensitive auditory sensors—also known as microphones!—throughout the house. These will pick up any noises you might make individually during the show. As well, there are cameras located all around the space, which will pick up any changes in your facial orientation or composition.

All of this represents a huge step forward in the production of theatre by quantifying the user experience without the mediation of intellect. We can now record the exact moment our artistry and your credulousness intersect. It's very exciting.

Now. We at Crow's take your privacy seriously. Please know that all data gathered are immediately anonymized, and no record is kept of an individual audience member's behaviours.

> [We switch to video, apparently a live shot of this audience. We zoom in on a single audience member (who looks uncomfortable), and we see a lightly pixellated box over their eyes.]

This is key. We don't need to know who you are; we need to know what's happening to you. We won't even count how many drinks you have at intermission! Our only goal at Crow's is to optimize the theatregoing experience for you.

> [A QR code comes up. Quite large.]

And listen: if all this makes you uncomfortable in any way, we hear you. We want you to enjoy your time here. If you for whatever reason wish not to participate in this information-gathering exercise—maybe you're shy, maybe you're on the lam from the law, we don't judge!—this QR code links to a form which will allow you to opt out of data gathering. Go ahead, we will take a brief pause in case you want to fill out that form.

[The head returns, now animated, and bobs around uncannily. He hums the Tom Tom Club sample from "Big Energy."]

By the way, there's a ten percent discount at the bar for people who don't opt out of our benign data-collection project.

The QR code actually links to a page that says: "Just kidding! We aren't harvesting your data. There are no sensors, microphones, or cameras. Enjoy the show."

Oh! While you've got your phones out! Our marketing department asks you to NOT turn them off during the show. I don't know why. Thank you very much!

[The head bloops and disappears.]

Blackout.

[What follows is a work of fiction.]

ACT ONE
SCENE ONE

In the black:

DOCTOROFF: Hey, guys. You know what I'm really, really good at?

Lights snap up. DOCTOROFF, FLEISSIG, DAVIS, VERNER, CAM. CAM *is looking at his laptop.*

Listening to people. I'm a listener.

FLEISSIG: Me too. So am—

DOCTOROFF: Working on the Olympic bid, for months I would just listen to people. Until I was blue in the face. People who hated the Olympics, people who couldn't care less, I listened to everyone. And by the time the bid was over, those people were all on side. And it worked, we got the Olympics. I mean, we didn't get the Olympics—who doesn't give New York City the Olympics a couple of years after 9/11?—the whole thing is so corrupt, I could tell you stories. We didn't get the Olympics, but it worked, my listening worked, in that all those people who hated the Olympics, now they were sorry we weren't getting the Olympics. This was all through my listening.

FLEISSIG: So glad to hear you say that, Dan. Public engagement is going to be crucial in this project.

DOCTOROFF: Public engagement is going to be crucial to the project, believe me. You listen to people, they talk, you listen, they feel heard, it's all crucial.

FLEISSIG: Agreed. But, so, the name is what we're—

DOCTOROFF: In fact, you can take an idea you heard, some random idea you heard with your listening, put it in the project, and then that guy goes: "Hey, that was my idea, I've been heard!" It's really marvellous.

FLEISSIG: Marvellous. And then, we've got all these people coming tomorrow, for the announcement, it would be great if the project had a name when we are announcing the project.

DOCTOROFF: My point is the project needs a name.

VERNER: Yes. I was thinking, maybe riffing off what Cam said—

CAM looks up like he's been shot.

CAM: Sorry?

VERNER: Sorry, no, I just meant—

CAM: Jane Jacobs?

VERNER: Did you find the quote?

CAM: Um, no, not yet.

VERNER: Okay. Sorry. Keep looking.

CAM goes back to his laptop.

DOCTOROFF: The name should have to do with listening. Like not this but: We Hear You Town.

FLEISSIG: What?

DOCTOROFF: Not that but that. The . . . Listening District.

FLEISSIG: Maybe we don't want to call a neighbourhood that's got surveillance all over it the Listening District.

CAM: *(staring at the laptop, mostly to himself)* It's not surveillance.

VERNER: *(simultaneously)* It's not surveillance.

VERNER and CAM look at each other.

DOCTOROFF: I just want people to feel seen.

FLEISSIG: We probably shouldn't emphasize they're being seen.

DOCTOROFF: Buy-in is crucial. When I was in the mayor's office, half of our work was about anticipating who was going to object to our zoning changes, and then meeting with them. And then you could add them to the list of people you've met with. As proof of your high level of engagement. Strategically, you guys need to start a list.

VERNER: Sure, but, that's a good idea, but today is about getting to tomorrow, the announcement of our project, and the project having a name.

FLEISSIG: Guys, you know what, actually—I really—there's a lot to do before tomorrow, I don't really have time for—

CAM: Here it is! I got it!

A beat.

No, sorry, that's not it.

FLEISSIG: Dan, sorry, I've got to, there's a lot of VIPs coming tomorrow, and I need to find, I dunno, chairs, get a microphone. Where do I—who's our microphone guy?

VERNER: Serge.

DOCTOROFF: All those people tomorrow, they need a name though. They need something to attach their imaginations to. That's basic. We need them all to be thrilled, to be hypnotized, and that starts with the name.

DAVIS: It's got a name.

DOCTOROFF: It, what?

DAVIS: The project has a name.

DOCTOROFF: No it doesn't.

DAVIS: Quayside.

DOCTOROFF: Oh, fuck. Of course. But that name sucks.

FLEISSIG: Guys—

DOCTOROFF: That just means dock. And it's fucked up, the spelling is fucked up. Quayside.

VERNER: The spelling is compelling.

DOCTOROFF: No successful development project in the history of the world ever started with a Q.

DAVIS: Queens Quay. That has two Qs.

DOCTOROFF: That's not a real—where is that?

DAVIS: A few hundred metres south of here.

DOCTOROFF: You guys still name things after Queen Elizabeth? Like what year is it!

DAVIS: Queen Victoria.

DOCTOROFF: That's even worse! But name a place that starts with Q outside of Toronto.

FLEISSIG: *(correcting him)* Toronto.

DOCTOROFF: What did I say?

FLEISSIG: Toronto.

DOCTOROFF: That's what I said.

FLEISSIG: Yes. That's wrong.

DOCTOROFF: I— What?

FLEISSIG: Don't say Toronto, say Toronto.

DOCTOROFF: Toe-ron— What??

VERNER: It doesn't matter.

FLEISSIG: Don't say the last T. Say Toronto.

DOCTOROFF: Ah. Toronto. Really?

FLEISSIG: Took me weeks to get that when I got here.

DOCTOROFF: *(saying it both ways)* Toronto. Toronto. Really?

FLEISSIG: Yes.

VERNER: It doesn't matter.

DOCTOROFF: Toronto. That feels weird. Isn't it disrespectful? Toronto?

TREE wanders on. TREE always addresses the audience.

FLEISSIG: Apparently not.

DAVIS: Can we—

FLEISSIG: Anyway, look, I've got to g—

CAM: I found it! "To approach a city as if it were just an architectural problem, capable of being given order by converting it into a disciplined work of art, is to make the mistake of substituting art for life. The results of such profound confusion between art and life are neither life nor art. They are taxidermy."

A beat.

VERNER: Ummm.

DOCTOROFF: What the fuck, Brad.

CAM: Yeah, sorry. I've just always loved that quote. For some reason I thought there might be a good name for the project in it.

DOCTOROFF: What, like Taxidermy Town? Jesus.

CAM: Still, it's a good quote, probably worth remem—

DOCTOROFF: Still, Jane Jacobs is fantastic. She lived here in Toronto, Torontò, whatever. Goddamn it. What about we call it Jane? The Jane District.

VERNER: Jane Lane? Jane Domain?

DAVIS: I like this idea as a tribute.

DOCTOROFF: She absolutely destroyed Robert Moses once. It was a highway or something. She beat his ass. This was in New York.

FLEISSIG: Yes.

DOCTOROFF: People have compared me to Robert Moses.

FLEISSIG: I mean, sure.

TREE: A bit of an exaggeration, but still, Dan Doctoroff presided over an era of extraordinary growth in New York City in the early aughts.

DOCTOROFF: I presided over an era of extraordinary growth in New York City in the early aughts.

FLEISSIG: No, I know.

TREE: The High Line, Hudson Yards, the Barclays Center.

DOCTOROFF: It's all in my book.

FLEISSIG: My thing is, Dan, we're announcing tomorrow and I have a lot to do.

DOCTOROFF: The book just came out. I'll get you a copy.

TREE: Doctoroff was deputy mayor to Michael Bloomberg. The Olympic bid allowed them to make changes to zoning laws and opened up a lot of underused land to development.

FLEISSIG: I have to go. The prime minister is coming. This can wait.

DOCTOROFF: The point of my book is: don't let others decide what constitutes your failure.

FLEISSIG: Like, I don't even know where he's going to sit.

DAVIS: Serge can help with seating.

FLEISSIG: Last time he was here for an announcement there was nowhere for him to sit down.

DAVIS: I know. We were so focused on the boat he came in on.

TREE: The gentrification of that era has made New York unlivable for most people.

DOCTOROFF: *(to TREE)* Reductive! We did some public housing too.

TREE: I read your book.

DOCTOROFF: *(to TREE)* Hey thanks!

TREE: It's possible I'm related to your book, but don't worry about that now.

DOCTOROFF: Did the Olympic bid fail? Maybe. But look what came out of it. Success after success.

TREE: And now Dan Doctoroff runs a company called Sidewalk Labs.

VERNER: How about we call it Keyside, but we spell it with a K? You know, a key unlocks the door to your new home, a key is loaded with possibilities, call it Keyside, with a K.

DOCTOROFF: Ugh, forget it. Ks are worse than Qs.

DAVIS: Okay, call it Quayside with a Q, but make the logo a key. Visual pun.

CAM: I like that. Visual pun.

FLEISSIG: Visual pun?

VERNER: Visual pun . . .

DAVIS: Visual pun.

DOCTOROFF: Visual puns are too much work. How about we call it Sidewalk?

FLEISSIG: What?

DOCTOROFF: Sidewalk.

DAVIS: That's your company's name.

DOCTOROFF: Correct. Half of it.

FLEISSIG: People are already going to be worried about this massive US corporation moving in and building in downtown Toronto.

TREE: Sidewalk Labs is a subsidiary of Alphabet. You've heard of Google?

> {The timeline comes to life. It starts at October 16, 2017, and swoops back to September 4, 1998, landing with a photo of Larry Page and Sergey Brin.}

DOCTOROFF: People are going to worry about a lot of things. Sometimes you have to ignore what people are worried about and do your thing. Let's just call it Sidewalk.

DAVIS: No.

CAM: How about this one? "Cities have the capability of providing something for everybody, only because, and only when, they are created by everybody."

DAVIS: *(to CAM)* That's a good one. Created by everybody. Is that Jane Jacobs too?

CAM: Yup. Maybe there's something in that? Inclusivity as city-building principle?

VERNER: Yes.

TREE: Google was founded in 1998 by these guys, Sergey Brin and Larry Page.

[A Google organizational chart appears; Brin and Page at the top as founders.]

VERNER: *They had a simple idea.*

DAVIS: YouCity. No, that's terrible.

DOCTOROFF: I'm telling you, Sidewalk. Just sit with Sidewalk a sec.

CAM: *Their idea was: you type a word into their search engine, and it showed you the most popular iterations of that word on the web.*

VERNER: *And then they had their next idea: to study user's choices with the hope of improving their algorithm.*

DAVIS: *Almost immediately, Page and Brin realized they could share the data they gathered from users with advertisers to make extremely focused ads.*

TREE: And now Google is worth about seven hundred billion dollars. The budget of the federal government of Canada is three hundred billion.

DAVIS: We're not calling it Sidewalk.

DOCTOROFF: Why not?

FLEISSIG: Because it's, it's, it's— It's dumb.

DOCTOROFF: Hey: don't knock dumb.

DAVIS: *Google's motto, from the time of its creation, was: Don't Be Evil.*

{"Don't Be Evil" appears on the timeline at early 2001.}

TREE: Investors forced the founders to hire a real CEO, someone with experience, and they chose this guy, Eric Schmidt.

[Schmidt appears on the org chart, above the other two.]

CAM: Here's another good one!

FLEISSIG: I don't have time for this.

I don't have time for this!

DAVIS: *Google, as you know, grew. Bought companies, developed mapping and email and cellphone software, all of which increased its ability to track user data.*

{The timeline whizzes through the aughts, past the launches of Gmail (April 1, 2004), Google Maps (February 8, 2005), and the acquisition of Android (July 2005).}

CAM: "It's bootless to try to harmonize commerce and government into one joint system of morality. The contradictions are innate, there is no way to escape them."

DOCTOROFF: Maybe that's enough Jane Jacobs.

TREE: I'm a tree? Don't worry about that right now.

DAVIS: *By 2010, Google was massive and Larry Page was restless. He felt the company had grown complacent and wanted it to return to the spirit of innovation that animated its founding. After meeting with Brin and Schmidt, it was agreed Page would take over as* CEO.

[On the org chart, Page moves up to CEO in 2010 and Schmidt moves to Executive Chairman.]

TREE: And then began the moon shots. X was a division of Google dedicated to wild ideas, innovations that would transform the world. Moon shots.

> [Names disappear from the org chart, and X appears as a division of Google.]

DOCTOROFF: *Robotics, AI, self-driving cars, all kinds of amazing shit.*

VERNER: *Some ideas grew into companies. Like Calico, devoted to anti-aging, or Wing, which was drones delivering freight.*

> [Wing, Calico, Verily, Fiber, Intrinsic, and DeepMind all populate the org chart below X.]

FLEISSIG: *Google was the only division making money.*

TREE: And in 2015, to separate the money-making stuff from the money-losing stuff, Google restructured as Alphabet.

> [Alphabet appears on top of the chart; Google takes its place among the other subsidiaries.]

DAVIS: *2015 was also the year the company officially abandoned "Don't Be Evil" as its motto.*

> {2015 ~~Don't Be Evil~~.}

VERNER: *Page started another division, Javelin, to engage in secret moon shots. Defence ideas, tubes to bike in, meatless meat.*

FLEISSIG: *He also became obsessed with the idea of building a city from the ground up.*

DOCTOROFF: *From the Internet up. What would a city look like if its basic infrastructure was digital? What efficiencies could be achieved?*

How would people move around, how would they work and play, and how much or how little government would this city need?

DAVIS: *If government services could pe provided algorithmically by a corporation, would government even be necessary?*

CAM: A *Javelin group was organized to come up with ideas. It quickly realized it needed to either build a city or take one over to get their ideas off the whiteboard.*

DAVIS: *The favourite idea was a floating city, at sea, built from scratch.*

TREE: A floating city, free of intrusive government, and covered in a protective dome.

VERNER: A *fucking dome.*

DAVIS: *Ugh, the dome.*

TREE: Eventually they had enough ideas—autonomous cars, digital tracking of citizens' choices, trash and delivery automation, the dome—it was time to make a company to pursue them.

{2015 Sidewalk Labs founded.}

FLEISSIG: *And they needed someone to run this new company.*

DOCTOROFF: *And there I was.*

FLEISSIG: *Hedge-fund rich, with plenty of city hall experience, Dan Doctoroff was great at city-building and turning a profit.*

DOCTOROFF: *What I am is a great listener.*

Hey, is Eric Schmidt going to be there tomorrow?

FLEISSIG: Yes. That's what I'm saying. The prime minister, Eric Schmidt, the mayor, the premier.

DOCTOROFF: The premier what?

VERNER: No, the lady who runs Ontario.

DOCTOROFF: And is Eric Schmidt going to be there tomorrow?

FLEISSIG: Yes!

DOCTOROFF: Oh! Great! And we're calling the project Sidewalk?

FLEISSIG, VERNER, & DAVIS: No!

DOCTOROFF: Okay, let's keep talking.

FLEISSIG: Dammit!

TREE: Sidewalk Labs was initially funded at three hundred million dollars.

DOCTOROFF: *I wanted them to give us two billion and turn us loose, but three hundred million was still enough to get going. We hired engineers, designers, urbanists, dozens of people like Brad here.*

CAM: Does he mean me?

VERNER: *(to DOCTOROFF)* His name is Cam.

DOCTOROFF: *We set up shop in New York. It was convenient.*

TREE: As they generated ideas, they had a problem: Larry Page was impatient.

DOCTOROFF: *Almost immediately we had to justify our existence to Larry. He wanted ideas, he wanted them big, and he wanted them now. I drove the company to come up with idea after idea.*

CAM: *Sidewalk created a catalogue of these ideas to keep Larry on the hook and excited. It was called the Yellow Book.*

FLEISSIG: Guys—

TREE: Everything was in the Yellow Book: the libertarian anti-government stuff, the stupid dome.

CAM: *By then Javelin had spent millions developing the dome idea—they had to include it.*

DOCTOROFF: *The Yellow Book was big, bright, and beautiful. Lots of pictures.*

TREE: Larry Page hated the Yellow Book.

FLEISSIG: Guys, I—

TREE: So almost immediately, Sidewalk Labs was under pressure to get a project off the ground.

DOCTOROFF: *And then we noticed Toronto.*

I think Sidewalk is a great name, and also funny, because I don't know if you're aware, but the plan is to not have actual sidewalks.

FLEISSIG: I HAVE TO GO.

FLEISSIG goes.

DOCTOROFF: Huh. That's my move.

VERNER: What is?

DOCTOROFF: Shouting and then walking out.

DAVIS: Will's under a lot of stress.

TREE: He is. That was Will Fleissig, CEO of Waterfront Toronto.

DAVIS: *Waterfront Toronto was created in 2001.*

VERNER: *After a failed Olympic bid.*

DOCTOROFF: *Really? I'll be damned.*

Okay, how about a bit of your name, a bit of ours: Sidewalk . . . Waterfront.

TREE: The idea was to capture the momentum created by the bid to finally revitalize Toronto's waterfront.

[A map of the Toronto waterfront.]

DAVIS: *Toronto used to stop at Front Street. That used to be the shore, but over the years, this was all filled in, this marshland, to house a booming shipping and industrial sector. Everything south of Front Street is man-made.*

[The eastern waterfront is highlighted on the map.]

TREE: That industry is all gone now, of course.

VERNER: *And what's there now amounts to the last underdeveloped waterfront land in North America.*

[The map zooms in on the Gardiner Expressway.]

TREE: That part right there is the Gardiner Expressway, a raised highway that cuts Toronto off from the lake in an extremely efficient way. Don't get me wrong, cars are great, I love cars, they feed me, don't worry about that right now, but from the moment it opened, before it opened, people realized the Gardiner was a kind of fuuucking hideous mistake. Waterfront Toronto's first recommendation in 2001 was that it be torn down.

[Photos of various projects appear: Sugar Beach, the Waterfront Innovation Centre, the Canary District.]

VERNER: *There was no way the City was going to tear down the Gardiner, so Waterfront Toronto got on with building things, finding developers to build the things they wanted, making parks, bit by bit fixing up the waterfront, carefully, and so, so very slowly. It's the Toronto way.*

DAVIS: *Our largest project to date is the naturalization of the mouth of the Don River.*

[Don River, mouth of the Don, Villiers Island.]

CAM: A *big problem with wanting to develop this part of the waterfront is that when they messed around with the shoreline a hundred years ago, they screwed up the mouth of this river right here, the Don. A river that empties into a big lake being forced to turn ninety degrees right at the end is no problem at all, unless it rains. It occasionally rains in Toronto, so Waterfront realized that they can't develop these nearby parts until they fix the screwed-up mouth of the Don.*

VERNER: *And this is how we're fixing it. Creating these channels to let the Don flow into the lake, and in the process creating this brand-new island. Villiers Island.*

DAVIS: *So all of this, the naturalization of this flood plain, the massive engineering and construction job that will create Villiers, the eventual development of some of this now safe-to-build-on land, we coordinated all those pieces in one project.*

TREE: And so now—

DOCTOROFF: *That is so interesting.*

TREE: What?

DOCTOROFF: *I just think that's amazing. I had no idea.*

CAM: *I put all this into a slide deck the week you hired me.*

DOCTOROFF: *Really? Can you send that to me?*

CAM: *I— Sure.*

DOCTOROFF: *Fascinating.*

VERNER: That was the last time the PM, premier, and mayor all showed up for an announcement. To announce funding for fixing the mouth of the Don. 1.5 billion dollars.

DAVIS: We brought them in by boat.

DOCTOROFF: Is there, there's no boat tomorrow, though, right?

DAVIS: No boat. Hopefully some chairs.

TREE: This is Meg Davis, Chief Development Officer at Waterfront Toronto.

VERNER: *Meg is a planner with an* MBA, *a ton of experience, and also a famous dad.*

TREE: And this is Kristina Verner, Vice President, Strategic Policy and Innovation for Waterfront Toronto.

DAVIS: *Kristina is a lecturer in cyberethics, has an* MBA, *and is an expert on the intersection of technology and urban design.*

TREE: And the next couple of years of their lives are going to absolutely suck.

VERNER: Pardon?

DAVIS: What's that?

TREE: Nothing. Look! Quayside!

[A photo with the Quayside site is highlighted.]

Quayside is a twelve-acre parcel at the foot of Parliament Street, its back up against the effing Gardiner Expressway, its face to the water. Nice little spot.

DAVIS: *Waterfront Toronto owns this land.*

VERNER: *And with the flood plain next door dealt with, we could finally think about how to develop it.*

DAVIS: *An agency like ours isn't driven by profit. So what could we do in the public interest with this choice piece of property?*

VERNER: *Climate change and affordability are the two greatest challenges facing cities. Could we use our twelve acres to test radical solutions to these massive problems?*

CAM: *Yes.*

DAVIS: *Can we make a carbon-neutral or even carbon-positive neighbourhood that's beautiful and accessible financially for a wide array of Torontonians?*

CAM: *Yes.*

VERNER: *Can we make discoveries here, and then use those discoveries in buildings and neighbourhoods in the future?*

CAM: *Yes.*

DAVIS: *This was our dream for Quayside.*

TREE: Verner and Davis held onto this dream for a decade before they could do anything about it.

VERNER: *But while we waited, we watched the twin crises of climate and affordability worsen, and we knew: get Quayside right, and the implications could be huge.*

DAVIS: *We knew we would need a partner with the expertise and resources to make something unmatched globally.*

DOCTOROFF: *And that's where Sidewalk Labs came in.*

TREE: Not so fast.

DAVIS: *We spent time consulting with various possible partners.*

VERNER: *We spoke with more than fifty companies. Including Sidewalk Labs.*

DOCTOROFF: *And we jumped at the chance to talk.*

TREE: Fun fact: Waterfront Toronto had to email Sidewalk Labs three times before you responded.

DOCTOROFF: *We eventually jumped at the chance.*

VERNER: *Then, once consultations were over, we created an* RFP*—a request for proposals.*

SCENE TWO

{March 2017.}

SIEMENS and QUAYSIDE EDGE JOINT VENTURE enter. DOCTOROFF takes his place beside them.

TREE: There were six initial respondents, whittled down to these three finalists. Siemens, a German-based digital communications company that had lots of experience in smart city ventures around the globe, and Quayside Edge Joint Venture, a Toronto-based consortium containing a builder, a retirement fund, and other finance companies.

DOCTOROFF: And me.

TREE: Yes, we'll get to you. The potential partners were asked to draw up a confidential response to Waterfront's RFP with their best ideas on sustainability and affordability.

DOCTOROFF: We leaked ours to the press.

TREE: Yes, you did.

DOCTOROFF: How could we not? It was a thing of beauty. Two hundred pages long, bright and shiny with a whole bunch of pictures.

TREE: Waterfront then held a series of day-long meetings with each proponent to dig into their proposals.

DOCTOROFF: It was like we were bidding for the Olympics all over again.

TREE: The process was overseen by a retired judge to ensure fairness. Okay. Hi!

SIEMENS: Hello, hi. At Siemens, we have a lot of experience collecting data and using it to optimize how a city works. Sensors placed throughout public spaces to measure foot traffic, cars and trucks, deliveries, and ice cream levels.

A beat.

SIEMENS: I am kidding about the last one.

TREE: Fantastic! And do you have any experience creating a digital layer in a completely new neighbourhood?

SIEMENS: Oh yes. A number of smart cities in Asia have used our tech.

TREE: Excellent. And, any experience as a builder?

SIEMENS: Of?

TREE: Buildings?

SIEMENS: Oh! Not as such, no.

TREE: Got it. Now—

DOCTOROFF: Now do me.

TREE: Just hang on. Quayside Joint Venture.

QUAYSIDE EDGE JOINT VENTURE: Quayside *Edge* Joint Venture.

TREE: Sorry, yes. You're a consortium.

QUAYSIDE EDGE JOINT VENTURE: Yes. I represent a retirement fund, Manulife Financial, and also Mattamy Homes, the premier residential builder in Ontario.

TREE: So you have financing and building covered. Do you have any experience using digital technologies to advance sustainability? As you know, we want Quayside to be a world leader in climate-friendly tech.

QUAYSIDE EDGE JOINT VENTURE: No, we don't have any direct experience doing that kind of stuff, but we figure we can engage some outside consultants to bring that aspect of the project to life.

TREE: I see. Do you have any consultants in mind for that? It's a brand-new field.

QUAYSIDE EDGE JOINT VENTURE: Actually, there's a company based in New York called Sidewalk Labs. We would probably approach them.

DOCTOROFF: *(shaking hands with* QUAYSIDE EDGE JOINT VENTURE*)* How ya doing.

TREE: Okay, and finally, Sidewalk Labs.

DOCTOROFF: Yes!

QUAYSIDE EDGE JOINT VENTURE: Oh.

TREE: So what experience do you have integrating tech and civic life?

DOCTOROFF: None.

TREE: None.

DOCTOROFF: None at all. Oh, hang on, we put up some on-street kiosks around New York City so that people could access the Internet.

TREE: I see.

DOCTOROFF: I'll give you one guess which part of the Internet people chose to access.

TREE: Ew.

DOCTOROFF: Correct. Anyway, in all seriousness, I'm Dan, CEO of Sidewalk Labs. Our mission is to build cities from the ground up—mobility, infrastructure, public realm, housing, governance, and financing. We're focused on meshing digital innovation with all those areas of life. The goal is always the improvement of quality of life—digital doesn't mean anything unless it helps some aspect of a resident's day-to-day. We have technologists on our staff, we have urbanists, and half of my job is trying to figure out how to get a technologist to talk to an urbanist.

TREE: Okay, that's actually . . . pretty good. Now, a question for all three: the next phase will involve a period of investigation and development, as well as community outreach. If you're the preferred proponent, will you be able to self-finance this period, which could be as long as eighteen months, prior to Waterfront entering into any kind of commitment?

SIEMENS: Eighteen months? Uh . . .

QUAYSIDE EDGE JOINT VENTURE: We actually just put this group together last week, so we haven't really discussed how we would manage the costs—

DOCTOROFF: We have fifty million dollars.

TREE: I beg your what?

DOCTOROFF: *(patting his breast pocket)* We have fifty million dollars.

TREE: Really.

QUAYSIDE EDGE JOINT VENTURE: Son of a—

SIEMENS: C'mon.

TREE: You're kidding.

DOCTOROFF: I don't kid. Bye, guys.

> *SIEMENS and QUAYSIDE EDGE JOINT VENTURE mulch off stage sadly.*

So. Let's get started.

SCENE THREE

{October 17, 2017.}

BURSTYN: Let's get started. Good morning! Thank you all for coming this morning. I'm happy to see all the dignitaries get chairs this time. I'm Helen Burstyn, chair of the board of Waterfront Toronto. We are delighted to announce we have found, in Sidewalk Labs, a partner to develop the eastern waterfront, starting with a new neighbourhood called Quayside.

TREE: Later, when the project started to go sideways, some people would return to today, to the morning of the original announcement, go over it forensically, to see if the seeds of the Quayside development's failure were apparent on this morning. For some, it was this off-the-cuff remark from the prime minister:

TRUDEAU: I'm extraordinarily pleased and excited to be here to welcome Eric Schmidt from Alphabet. Eric and I have been talking about collaborating on this for a few years now.

TREE: If you wanted to claim Trudeau rigged the selection process in Sidewalk Lab's favour, you used that remark to prove it. This unscripted remark from Premier Kathleen Wynne about noisy protestors outside the building would prove to be prophetic:

WYNNE: We are here this morning, an exciting announcement to make, and with the backdrop of democracy. We are blessed.

TREE: Which she followed up with:

WYNNE: There will be challenges along the way. We will confront them together.

TREE: There were challenges along the way. We did not confront them together. Some people found Toronto Mayor John Tory's relentless, almost needy boosterism indicative of Canada's eagerness to enter into a deal with Google without understanding the costs:

TORY: With the choice that Sidewalk Labs has made today, I see this as a time of huge confidence in Toronto and in Canada. To have the Sidewalk team working hand in hand with us will surely confirm our status as *the* global centre for urban innovation.

TREE: An assertion he then repeated in his brutal French:

TORY: Je suis fier de Toronto de vien le premier ville Mondial pour l'innovation urban. Nous travaillerons main dans la main avec Sidewalk et la résultat sera spectaculaire.

TREE: Wow, sorry. Some thought this obvious joke from Eric Schmidt was serious and laid bare Google's imperialist plans:

SCHMIDT: Our founders, years ago, got really excited at the idea of taking all the technical things that we know and applying them to cities. They kept talking about all of the things we could do if someone would just give us a city and put us in charge. Mmm, that's not how it works, guys! For all sorts of really good reasons!

TREE: But if you really wanted to understand where the seeds of the coming misfortune lay, they were here, in Dan Doctoroff's remarks:

DOCTOROFF: We looked all over the world for the perfect place to bring this vision to life, and we found it here in Toronto.

TREE: That statement, which takes the fact that Toronto chose Sidewalk and flips it on its head to make it sound like Sidewalk chose Toronto, was a perfect encapsulation of the trouble to come.

DOCTOROFF: That's the statement you have a problem with? C'mon, people actually applauded when I said that.

TREE: It's true. People applauded. A reminder that Toronto has never, not once, ever, been cool about anything.

DOCTOROFF: How about my Jane Jacobs quote that day?

TREE: Yeah, we're not doing tha—

DOCTOROFF: She wrote: " . . . as a relatively recent transplant from New York, I am frequently asked whether I find Toronto sufficiently exciting. I find it almost too exciting." She said, "Here is the most hopeful and healthy city in North America."

TREE: Okay, thanks.

DOCTOROFF: My guy Brad found that for me.

SCENE FOUR

Waterfront Toronto boardroom. VERNER *and* CAM. CAM *wears a Pavement* T*-shirt under his suit jacket.*

CAM: He still thinks my name is Brad.

VERNER: Amazing.

CAM: I've been with the company for eight months. He hired me himself. The first job he gave me was I had to shred hundreds of copies of the Yellow Book.

VERNER: Was it as crazy as everyone says?

CAM: Oh yeah. One of my favourite ideas in there was they would offer greater access to your own neighbourhood based on how much data you were willing to give up.

VERNER: No way! That's so gross! Now I want to read the whole thing.

CAM: I saved a copy. I'll show you sometime.

VERNER: Ooo, yes please.

CAM: It has hundreds of pictures of domes. Domes covering city blocks. Domes covering whole neighbourhoods.

DAVIS *enters.*

DAVIS: Hi. Sorry, am I late?

VERNER: No no.

CAM: We were a little early, I think.

(to VERNER) Anyway, I'll bring it in. Some of the ideas are good for loosening up your brain.

VERNER: He stole a copy of the Yellow Book!

DAVIS: Really!

VERNER: It's all domes all day.

CAM: The dome is objectively stupid, but it's Larry Page's favourite idea.

DAVIS: Is that where the building raincoats in your RFP response come from? They're sort of dome-y.

CAM: Close enough for Larry, we hope. Fifty percent of our time is spent making sure Alphabet stays happy.

VERNER: Until Sidewalk Labs can do something, turn a profit, become a real boy?

CAM: Yeah. Everyone has to please someone to get things done.

You guys are sort of in the same position.

DAVIS: What do you mean?

CAM: Maybe I'm out of line, but Waterfront Toronto has a twenty-year mandate that's just about to come up. A big, exciting project like Quayside is exactly the kind of thing that gets one's mandate extended, no?

DAVIS: You've . . . done some research.

CAM: Of course.

There's a real tightrope Sidewalk is on with this project. In our RFP response to you, where we suggest all these innovative ideas, every idea is based on tech that already exists. Some things, like the garbage robots, are extreme examples of existing tech, but none of it is brand-new. How could it be? We haven't gotten here yet, haven't done any research, haven't identified problems. All we did was try to win a competition.

VERNER: Which is why your RFP response managed to be both two-hundred pages long and short on details.

CAM: But at the same time, Sidewalk has to make it sound like every idea is revolutionary, a brand-new invention, to keep Larry Page interested.

VERNER: That's a weird position to be in.

CAM: Yeah. I'm sure I just violated five different parts of the NDA I signed.

VERNER: You're a bad man, Brad.

CAM: Mmm hmm. Damn right I am.

A pause. DAVIS *looks at the two of them carefully.*

DAVIS: What's going on?

VERNER: Hmm?

DAVIS: Was that . . . flirting?

CAM: Flirting! What?

VERNER: Meg!

A beat.

Where were we?

CAM: The ummm public consultations?

VERNER: Yes, the public consultations. Waterfront will run the first public presentation November first. It'll feature Will and Dan. Then Sidewalk will run the one next May, then we'll co-host the one next August. The one in December of next year we will figure out when we get closer to it.

Helen BURSTYN *walks by, sees them talking, pauses, then goes.*

CAM: Okay, can I just say: Is it wise to have so much public consultation when there's nothing to show people yet?

DAVIS: Possibly not. But it's in Waterfront's DNA. We consult the public on every project.

CAM: Well, secrecy is in Sidewalk's DNA, so this will be interesting.

DAVIS: How did you end up at Sidewalk?

VERNER: Yeah. You don't immediately come off as Google-creepy, Brad.

CAM: Why you're so kind, thank you very much.

VERNER: Not at all.

Another beat.

DAVIS: Should I . . . leave?

VERNER: No no. How did you end up at Sidewalk?

CAM: I took urban design at UC Berkeley, and after I graduated I worked at a couple of different architects in Maryland. Low-level stuff, barely making enough to cover my student loans. My uncle's a corporate lawyer in New York. He met Dan Doctoroff when he was in the mayor's office. My uncle got me the interview. When I got hired I was one of the few people in the office who knew where Toronto was, so I got sent up here in the first wave.

DAVIS: So, Cam, can I ask, obviously off the record, from your perspective, is what we're trying to do here, um, what do you think, are we being—

VERNER: Meg is shy. She wants to ask if you think Quayside is a terrible idea.

DAVIS: No, I was just— Okay, yes.

CAM: Meg: this project is ridiculous.

DAVIS: Oh, uh, okay.

CAM: It's going to be amazing!

DAVIS: Oh! Okay!

> [Renderings of the Quayside project are shown: Parliament Slip, the streets, light rail, small autonomous cars.]

CAM: I can't believe I get to work on this. Three million square feet of housing, retail, and public space. The water! The chance to open up the slip, bring people to it, play with where the land ends and the lake begins.

The chance to make streets that are for people. A variety of transportation options all blended thoughtfully and human-centred. A place that's ready for autonomous vehicles when they arrive. I know people roll their eyes at autonomous vehicles, but they're incredibly docile. If there have to be cars in the area, let them be cars that move according to rules that make it impossible to run someone down.

Streets that are flexible—depending on time of day, sidewalks that grow or shrink, widen to become plazas, places to hang out.

> [Building exteriors, the raincoats.]

I know you think the raincoats are dumb, and maybe they *are* just vestigial dome bullshit. I mean, they're just awnings that go all the way down to the sidewalk. The idea is to extend the outdoor seasons as long as possible by protecting people from the worst of the weather. Toronto has a massive system of underground tunnels in the downtown core to avoid the weather. How much nicer would it be to stay at street level?

> [Modular units being connected to a building spine. Cutaways of small units, larger family units, light-industry units.]

But it's the buildings that really get me going. The most successful buildings from the last century are the lofts. First industrial, then they were used for retail, then residential. That's the kind of long-term flexibility we're going for. Modular units created off-site and put into place means the building goes up in half the time and at two thirds the cost. Crazy Japanese mushroom insulation, safer and completely sustainable, and electricity that's completely safe because it's delivered along an Ethernet cable, not via copper that's buried inside a wall, waiting to short out and start a fire.

Walls without utilities inside them mean they can be moved or removed more easily. A one-bedroom becomes a two-bedroom when you have another kid. Back to a one-bedroom when you get old and want to age in place.

> [Tall timber buildings, wooden interiors.]

And the whole thing, the whole building made of locally sourced, locally manufactured timber. The carbon in the harvested wood is put in these buildings and trapped for a hundred years. Create a supply chain of sustainable timber, from growth through manufacturing to building, and you're taking carbon out of the atmosphere. We can make thirty-storey buildings out of wood, and those buildings are actually harder to burn down than if they were made of concrete.

[Local power generation, with the waste and delivery facilities under the buildings. Then back out to the streetscape.]

The neighbourhood will generate its own geothermal power and can maybe export the excess to other neighbourhoods. Building is cheaper so the housing can be cheaper to rent or own. It's beautiful, you can live a lifetime here, you can work here, and you know what? This is going to be the only way to make housing soon. Toronto is exploding, hundreds of thousands of people are moving here at a moment when the planet's on fire. Our only choice is to make cities that don't produce carbon. You guys are so lucky. You're so smart. This place, Quayside, is going to be—it's going to be—this is how we are going to have to do it. There's really no other way . . .

VERNER: Cam?

DAVIS: Cam, are you . . . crying?

CAM: *(yes he is)* No.

VERNER: Cam!

DAVIS: Oh!

CAM: Shut up.

VERNER: Oh! You love Quayside!

CAM: Okay, shut up.

VERNER: *(this is the hottest thing she's ever seen)* You big fuckin' baby!

CAM: Anyway. Happy to be here.

Helen BURSTYN *appears at the door.*

BURSTYN: Hi.

VERNER: Helen! Hi.

DAVIS: This is Cam Malagaam from Sidewalk.

VERNER: We were finalizing the schedule for the public consults. This is Helen Burstyn, chair of our board.

BURSTYN: Hi. Great to meet you. Could you . . . ? We need the . . .

CAM: Oh! Yes.

CAM *packs up.*

DAVIS: See you 1:30 to discuss the parking pilot.

CAM: Great. Great to meet you.

He goes.

BURSTYN: Hi.

VERNER & DAVIS: Hi.

BURSTYN: He was here yesterday.

VERNER: Yes. Sidewalk doesn't have office space yet, so Will's letting him work here. It's mostly meetings, mostly with us, so it seemed simpler. Do you need the boardroom?

BURSTYN: No. I— Here's the thing. He's from Sidewalk.

DAVIS: Yes.

BURSTYN: Look, I know you're working with him, but he can't be here.

VERNER: It's just for now. We're still working out how exactly this collaboration is going to function—

BURSTYN: We're not collaborating with Sidewalk Labs. Not yet. We're negotiating with Sidewalk Labs. And until that negotiation is complete, no one from Sidewalk in our space, okay?

VERNER: Understood.

DAVIS: Of course.

BURSTYN: Thank you. I'll speak to Will.

DAVIS: Is everything going okay?

BURSTYN: I'm not sure. It's a very different culture over there. They're a little . . . pushy.

VERNER: I've noticed.

BURSTYN: And there's a pretty big tide of Google-loathing that's coming our way. The press is so far almost uniformly bad.

DAVIS: Yes.

BURSTYN: I think Will is a little overwhelmed.

FLEISSIG wanders on stage at the St. Lawrence Centre.

FLEISSIG: Are we? Hi, guys, are we starting?

(to audience) Hi, sorry, I was told we were starting. One sec.

He looks off stage.

BURSTYN: And also the City hates us.

FLEISSIG: Hi, everyone, I'm Will Fleissig, CEO of Waterfront Toronto. I don't know where everyone is . . .

DAVIS: Why?

BURSTYN: City staff is mad we let Sidewalk publish its RFP response.

DAVIS: We didn't *let them* do anything.

BURSTYN: Sidewalk had pictures of the Port Lands in the doc, implying that they'll be involved all across the waterfront.

FLEISSIG: Anyway, maybe we can just get started. I'm Will Fleissig.

BURSTYN: But of course, the City has its own plan for the Port Lands. And it definitely doesn't involve Sidewalk Labs.

FLEISSIG: What an incredible turnout!

DAVIS: Not a great moment to have City staff against us.

BURSTYN: Exactly. So. Lots of fires to put out before we start any new ones.

DAVIS: Got it.

FLEISSIG: Oh! Hang on.

He fiddles with the mic pack he's wearing, turns on his mic.

SCENE FIVE

FLEISSIG: Hello? Ah, that's better. Hi. Hello. Okay.

{November 1, 2017.}

DOCTOROFF comes on.

DOCTOROFF: Hi, sorry, I had to take a call.. Hello! Wow! What a turnout!

FLEISSIG: I know.

DOCTOROFF: I gotta tell you, when I was in the Bloomberg administration we changed zoning for forty percent of Manhattan, and we had to have all these public meetings, which were great of course, but man, we never had a turnout like this.

FLEISSIG: This is Dan Doctoroff, he's the CEO of Sidewalk Labs.

DOCTOROFF: Correct. Hey, everybody.

FLEISSIG: And as we established, I'm Will Fleissig, CEO of Waterfront Toronto.

DOCTOROFF: Correct.

FLEISSIG: Just to introduce myself further, I became CEO two years ago, and before that I managed the creation of a neighbourhood called West Village at UC Davis, the largest zero-net-energy community in the United States.

DOCTOROFF: But you live here now.

FLEISSIG: Yes I do.

DOCTOROFF: That's so cool! Anyway, in all seriousness, I'm Dan, CEO of Sidewalk Labs. Our mission is to build cities from the ground up—mobility, infrastructure, public realm, building, governance, and financing. We're focused on meshing digital innovation with all those areas of life. The goal is always the improvement of quality of life—digital doesn't mean anything unless it helps some aspect of a resident's day-to-day. We have technologists on our staff, we have urbanists, and half of my job is trying to figure out how to get a technologist to talk to an urbanist.

FLEISSIG: I bet. At Waterfront, we—

DOCTOROFF: So we looked all over the world to try to find a place to build out a city the way we knew we could. And you know what? Of all the places we looked at, we thought the best place was Toronto. Your diversity, your inclusiveness? Incredible. And the rapid growth here means that people might be just a little desperate, or should I say open, to trying new things.

FLEISSIG: To be clear, we selected Sidewalk, Sidewalk didn't choose Toronto.

DOCTOROFF: Absolutely. Toronto is going to be an amazing host city.

FLEISSIG: Maybe the term "host," maybe that's not great, host, it kind of sounds like you guys are going to come bursting out of Toronto's chest.

DOCTOROFF: Ha ha, maybe! You know, Sigourney Weaver is from New York.

FLEISSIG: The point is, we had a long process to find an innovation and financing partner. It was an open competition, there was a retired judge who oversaw the process, and Sidewalk came out on top.

DOCTOROFF: We're very grateful. We're bringing all of our experience, and also fifty million dollars. Which we will be using over the course of the next year to connect with Toronto, learn about Toronto, and listen to what Toronto wants in a new neighbourhood. By the way, let's all just take a sec and appreciate that I know how to pronounce Toronto.

FLEISSIG: It's fantastic. And at the end of this year-long process, Waterfront Toronto can back out of the deal. We can say thanks, Sidewalk, but what you're proposing is not for us.

DOCTOROFF: Of course. We are going to spend the next year humble, listening, and offering ideas.

FLEISSIG: And at the end of the process, whatever plan we come up with will still need to go through all the federal, provincial, and local regulatory regimes.

DOCTOROFF: Yes, except of course the beauty of an agency like Waterfront Toronto is, because it's a creature of all three levels of government, it can expedite all those things, streamline the process for us.

FLEISSIG: What? No we can't.

DOCTOROFF: What?

FLEISSIG: What?

DOCTOROFF: Waterfront Toronto was made by all three levels of government, yes?

FLEISSIG: Yes.

DOCTOROFF: And you therefore manage all the regulatory stuff in-house, yes?

FLEISSIG: No.

DOCTOROFF: No?

FLEISSIG: Waterfront Toronto has none of those powers.

DOCTOROFF: Well. Shit. What powers does it have?

FLEISSIG: Can we maybe discuss this later?

DOCTOROFF: Like, any powers at all?

FLEISSIG: Later.

DOCTOROFF: Okay. But shit.

FLEISSIG: Okay! So I think we should discuss a couple of things that have come up the last few days, and then we'll open the floor to questions. After that, there are members of both our teams at the back and in the lobby who can take your comments, questions, whatever you've got. The first thing I know on people's minds is privacy. There will be sensors on site to manage traffic, waste, energy use, and very possibly other things too. Dan, can you tell people what steps you propose to keep people's identities private in those circumstances? Dan?

DOCTOROFF: So, instead of helping us deal with three levels of government, Waterfront is basically a fourth level?

FLEISSIG: Dan. Privacy?

DOCTOROFF: Okay. Well. On privacy, we're going to follow something called Privacy By Design. It's a protocol developed by Ann Cavoukian—she was the privacy commissioner here in Ontario. The idea is all data is anonymized at source, meaning at the sensor. So instead of taking a picture of you walking across the street, you're just a blob. An unidentifiable blob crossing the street.

FLEISSIG: Obviously, this is going to be an ongoing conversation to build out the protocols and structures around privacy. We are putting together a committee of data experts called the Digital Strategy Advisory Panel in the new year to help us look at all the proposals as they come in. There are other pieces here, like deciding how data gets stored, who has access to it.

DOCTOROFF: Will, let me just address the elephant in the room, which is Google. We will never, ever sell data collected at Quayside to anyone. Full stop. We're here, we're doing this, and obviously we're spending a lot of money to be here, and should we go ahead, should you let us do so, we feel like there's plenty of other ways to make plenty of money with this project. We're a for-profit company, sure, but data sales isn't part of our business plan.

FLEISSIG: The next thing, and then we'll open it up to questions, is there have been reports in the news criticizing us for keeping our deal secret. The deal we signed a couple of weeks ago was an agreement to agree. That's all. We committed to putting together a more comprehensive deal in six weeks' time. Once that deal is worked out, we will release both deals to the public. But remember, even after that, Waterfront can still walk away.

DOCTOROFF: We're going to miss that deadline, by the way.

FLEISSIG: Probably.

DOCTOROFF: Definitely. By a lot.

FLEISSIG: Anyway, as soon as we complete it, we'll release it.

DOCTOROFF: Absolutely.

FLEISSIG: Now, let's take some questions. If you have one, head over to the mics we have set up on either side. Yes, you, sir, go ahead, identify yourself and maybe let us know what part of town you're from.

TIM: Hi, I'm Tim, and I live over on King Street West. My question is about transit. There is none in that neighbourhood. How in the hell, excuse my language, but how in the hell do you expect the TTC, the City, to build the LRT across to this new neighbourhood? There's no money for it. How can you have a sustainable neighbourhood with no mass transit?

FLEISSIG: Great question. We think—

DOCTOROFF: I got this, Will. It's a great story from my book, Tom, I don't know if you've read it. We needed to build a new subway stop to service Hudson Yards, but the City was broke and the state refused to pay for it. So what we did was this: we sold bonds to investors, who only got paid if the property taxes in the area went up after the subway was put in. So now they get an excellent return on their money, paid out of the incremental difference in property taxes between what they were and what they are now that the neighbourhood is fancy—it's quite a fancy neighbourhood.

FLEISSIG: To be clear, we aren't currently entertaining ideas that involve tax money getting diverted from the City and going to bondholders. No one is saying that.

DOCTOROFF: But we could be saying that. There are innovative financing solutions, is my point.

FLEISSIG: Next question? Yes. Hi.

BIANCA: Hi, my name is Bianca Wylie, I live in the west end. My questions is this: Why is it necessary to involve a foreign-owned corporation in the creation of tech for a new development when we have the expertise in-house in government to tackle the problems of climate change and affordable housing? The problem with public/private partnerships is that one partner is always out to maximize profit, and so public money is inevitably spent helping the corporation achieve that goal. Jane Jacobs said that government and business, because they exist in different moral paradigms, are incompatible. Why aren't we doing this ourselves instead of involving a company that's renowned for taking, in some cases stealing, people's data for its own use?

DOCTOROFF: Definitely lots to unpack there. Will?

FLEISSIG: Hi, Bianca, we've spoken before, and I'm sure we will again. I think you're asking some very important questions about Quayside in the press and on the Internet, and your expertise and how much you care about Toronto's future are really evident. To your question: Waterfront doesn't have the expertise or resources to achieve what we want to achieve with Quayside on our own. We don't want to use existing solutions; we want to create new ones. Our experience is that governments are evolutionary thinkers, not revolutionary thinkers. Which is probably for the best.

You're right to be skeptical of public/private partnerships. Sometimes they work out and sometimes they don't. But the fact is, they're how most big things get done these days. Waterfront Toronto is a public entity, in a unique position as owner of this land, and without the need to exploit it strictly for profit, we can try here to do something in the public interest by pushing the limits of what's possible while also making something beautiful. And we have a lot of backstops in our process to make sure our intentions are paramount at Quayside and not Sidewalk Lab's desire for profit.

DOCTOROFF: It's our job to give you what you want and to figure out how to make money doing it.

FLEISSIG: Yes, but, emphasis on the first part.

DOCTOROFF: And the second!

BIANCA: You can see why everyone is nervous.

FLEISSIG: Listen, I get it, I do. I think the only way here is to be open and transparent with the public at each step of the process.

BIANCA: In that case, why won't you release the deal you signed with Sidewalk Labs?

FLEISSIG: As I said—

DOCTOROFF: We will, we're going to, we're committed to that. Yes! Question over here.

GORD: Hi, I'm Gord, and I'm from Mississauga. I've had a look at the Sidewalk Labs document, and a lot of it seems pretty good. I'm not sure how I feel about getting charged whenever I throw out a piece of plastic, and I have a question about how my privacy is protected and yet you know it's me that threw out that plastic.

TREE walks on.

But that's not my question. My question is: the tall timber buildings. You want to build like thirty storeys. They'd be the tallest wooden buildings in the world. But currently they're only approved for six storeys in Toronto. How will you get around the City's rules about maximum heights and all the other regulatory things you're going to have to do? And down the road? If you want to build elsewhere on the waterfront? How are you going to get the City to change its plan for the Port Lands to get that done?

FLEISSIG: It's our hope that success at Quayside will change how the rest of the eastern waterfront gets developed.

DOCTOROFF: We're confident we can work with the City to amend the rules that need to be amended.

TREE: You're dreaming.

DOCTOROFF: Don't forget, I worked eight years as deputy mayor of New York. We rezoned forty percent of the city to do what we wanted to do. So I understand how to get things done and handle the local bureaucracy, force bureaucratic change when it's important.

SCENE SIX

TREE: You have no idea what you're talking about, big guy. I'm here to show you all just how delusional Dan's optimism about handling Toronto City staff was.

[Visuals throughout the following: United Empire Loyalists, Family Compact, Muddy York, etc.]

Toronto was founded and built by a bunch of British people that didn't want to be American. It was a centre of trade and dominated by Protestants who valued the preservation of order over everything. Their order. The politics of the town reflected this connection between business interests and political power. And still do.

[Mayor John Tory on the Rogers advisory board @ $100,000/ year https://globalnews.ca/news/9024927 /torontos-integrity-commissioner-to-investigate-mayor -john-tory-over-ties-to-rogers/.]

[https://www.theglobeandmail.com/opinion /article-canadas-telecom-family-compact-wins-again/.]

In 2002, after a period of wild growth and then amalgamation, things got a little loose at city hall for fifteen seconds. A city councillor took kickbacks on a computer-leasing deal. The computer salesman was also boning the City's treasurer at the time. A bit of a mess.

[Computer scandal headlines including: https://www.cbc.ca /news/canada/inquiry-judge-people-disgraced -themselves-in-toronto-scandal-1.548496.]

After that, staff at Toronto City Hall went to extraordinary lengths to make sure that kind of thing could never happen again. The building became a monument to rule-following, and a kind of bureaucratic complexity that made elected officials heavily dependent on City staff.

Now: How best to illustrate this? With me. I'm a tree, like I said, and my name is Glen Woods. My name isn't Glen Woods, I don't know why I said that. That's just two more words for a group of trees. I don't have a name, I'm a tree.

> [City council meeting December 5, 2017, part one of two starts running at 1:51:36. https://www.youtube.com/watch?v=rgtnt599rjM.]

I'm a Norway maple, and I reside at 134 Yorkminster Road. You know what Toronto homeowners are really into? Cutting down trees. But: Did you know that if you want to commit arboricide on your own property in the City of Toronto, you have to get the City's permission? And if City staff says no, you may not cut down your tree. And you want to appeal, the appeal is debated by and voted on by the ENTIRE CITY COUNCIL.

SPEAKER NUNZIATA: Next item is NY26.39; application to remove a private tree at 134 Yorkminster Road.

TREE: That's me!

SPEAKER NUNZIATA: Councillor Robinson?

COUNCILLOR JAYE ROBINSON: On behalf of the resident at 134 Yorkminster Road, I just want to ask Urban Forestry staff why they are recommending against the removal of this tree, given the homeowner states its root system is damaging the sewer line on the property?

URBAN FORESTRY STAFF: Madam Speaker, through you, the tree in question is 3.6 metres from the municipal sewer line, its roots currently pose no threat to it, and in the past the homeowner has claimed the tree was interfering with a fence, which it does not; we believe the homeowner wants to install a hot tub on the site, and that's the source of the request for tree removal.

COUNCILLOR JAYE ROBINSON: I see. Okay.

SPEAKER NUNZIATA: Recorded vote on NY26.39.

TREE: Toronto, a city of three million residents and countless trees, drops whatever it's doing and debates the existence of a single tree.

> [The recorded vote on the Norway maple at 134 Yorkminster Rd., 1:53:05.]

SPEAKER NUNZIATA: The item carries, thirty to six. The tree is spared.

TREE: Yes! Suck it, homeowner at 134 Yorkminster Road! Fuck your hot tub!

I share with you the greatest day of my life so far to illustrate the iron grip the Toronto City bureaucracy has on life here. It will come up later. And Doctoroff and the whole team at Sidewalk had no idea. They spent their time lobbying elected officials, believing they were the path to cutting the hundred corners necessary to getting something done. They didn't even realize that the mayor is just one vote on council; he doesn't run the city.

DOCTOROFF: *(popping on)* He what? The mayor what? He's just one vote?

TREE: Yeah. Sorry.

DOCTOROFF: Son of a—! How do you guys get anything done!

TREE: An excellent question.

DOCTOROFF: *(exiting)* Sheeezuz.

TREE: Sidewalk and Waterfront were already in the doghouse with City staff before the project was announced. Staff hated that the flashy Sidewalk RFP response document was leaked to the press.

This is an email from David Stonehouse, Director of the Waterfront Secretariat, City of Toronto:

STONEHOUSE: We were very clear with WT and Sidewalk Labs Thursday that we did not want the proposal document released this week and that it needs a thorough review by City staff.

TREE: The problem was that the document contained one picture of the company's plans outside of Quayside, in the Port Lands. One picture.

[Graphic from the RFP response.]

But the City, you see, has its own official plan for the Port Lands. A plan it is very fond of. A plan it has no interest in deviating from. This, from the city's economic development manager Michael Williams in the same email thread:

WILLIAMS: Just to reiterate, it is "not now, not ever" because of how different it is from the City's vision of what is to happen in the Port Lands.

DAVIS, FLEISSIG, and VERNER enter a Bay Street boardroom.

TREE: There was nothing City staff could do about Quayside because Waterfront owns the site. But it was going to make damn sure Waterfront's vision didn't bleed into the rest of the neighbourhood.

["The real jungle is in the office of the bureaucrats."
—Jane Jacobs]

SCENE SEVEN

{Spring 2018.}

DOCTOROFF, Micah LASHER, and a grey, silent lawyer enter the Bay Street boardroom. Hands are shaken, except for the lawyer, who sits apart.

DOCTOROFF: Good morning, all. Thanks for coming. This is Micah Lasher, Sidewalk's policy and communications guy.

LASHER: Hi, guys.

DOCTOROFF: We worked together at City Hall. So, as you well know, we are way overdue to get an agreement on—

FLEISSIG: 'Scuse me, Dan, but who is that?
(waves at the lawyer, who does not respond) Hi!

DOCTOROFF: That's just a lawyer. Now—

DAVIS: Hang on, you brought a lawyer to this meeting?

DOCTOROFF: I guess so? Now: the first thing we have to discuss, before we get into this agreement, is the controversy surrounding communications.

VERNER: Yes, it's very simple: you should not be putting out press releases or talking to the press, because that's our job.

LASHER: No it isn't.

FLEISSIG: Listen, I get that this is a new position for you guys—

LASHER: No it isn't.

FLEISSIG: I just mean, look, you're a vendor. We've selected you. It's our practice that all communications flow through Waterfront Toronto.

LASHER: We're not going to ask for permission to talk about our project.

DAVIS: Whose project?

FLEISSIG: I'm afraid I'm going to have to insist that we release communications jointly, or not at all.

DOCTOROFF: I think we should circle back to that question at a later date. It's complex.

VERNER: Now hang on. We're the lead in this partnership. I don't really know how to say it more clearly. Will?

FLEISSIG: Uh, yeah. That's, yeah.

DOCTOROFF: No, sure.

A pause.

DAVIS: Waterfront is prepared to walk away from our arrangement if we can't agree on communications.

FLEISSIG: I mean, we're not going to walk away over comms, but you know. Guys, c'mon.

LASHER: I think we can find wording on a joint comms strategy.

DAVIS: There is no strategy. You don't speak unless we speak together.

A pause.

DOCTOROFF: Okay. We agree. Now—

VERNER: Hang on. We know that in the last fifteen days you've met with the mayor twice, with three different city councillors, you've taken separate meetings with people in the premier's office, and with the provincial innovation minister. You've met with local residents Catherine Rutherford, Andy Gibson, and Preet Gill.

LASHER: How do you know all that?

DAVIS: That's not important.

FLEISSIG: The point is: Why on earth are you having meetings here in Toronto without us?

LASHER: Well, why not?

VERNER: Why not?

DOCTOROFF: We have our own work to do here to get to know people, to bring them on side with our vision, to project an air of focus, of energy, determination.

VERNER: There is no conceivable reason for you to be meeting with government officials, with any stakeholders, on what is fundamentally our project.

LASHER: There is no goddamn way we're going to clear our meeting schedule with you.

A beat.

With respect.

VERNER: Hey, well with respect, fuck you.

FLEISSIG: Hey, hey, okay! Oooooookay now.

DAVIS: If you meet with a stakeholder again, even one more time, without our knowledge, we will terminate our agreement. Clear?

DOCTOROFF: Yes.

DAVIS: Micah, are we clear about this?

LASHER: Of course.

FLEISSIG: Okay. So, to the actual purpose for this meeting. We are, as you know, now several months late signing the Plan Development Agreement. The absence of the agreement has not only slowed down our collaborative work, but it has created a vacuum into which the public has put all its various anxieties about our partnership and the project as a whole.

LASHER: You're describing a comms vacuum. Which we can help with.

VERNER: We're dealing with it. People hear Google, people freak out. We're handling it.

LASHER: Are you though? Because . . .

VERNER: *(to DAVIS)* I swear to god, I'm going to fucking lose it in a sec.

A beat. The lawyer makes a note.

DOCTOROFF: I agree that we need to sign off on the Plan Development Agreement ASAP. What's the problem?

DAVIS: The problem is that you keep putting in language that guarantees Sidewalk Labs more land than the Quayside parcel, and we keep taking it out.

LASHER: You should stop doing that then.

FLEISSIG: Our agreement is for twelve acres. That's it.

DOCTOROFF: Hang on, everything we ever heard about this is that Quayside is just the beginning, that the long-term plan is to develop all of the eastern waterfront.

FLEISSIG: It is, but—

LASHER: Your prime minister said it. Your premier. The mayor. Everyone talked not just about Quayside, but beyond.

DOCTOROFF: Your own RFP mentions the Port Lands three times on the first page.

LASHER: It mentions the Port Lands *before* it mentions Quayside.

FLEISSIG: Okay, but—

DOCTOROFF: Will, did you promise us something you had no right to promise?

A beat.

FLEISSIG: I never said further development would be guaranteed. I never said that.

LASHER: You sure?

DOCTOROFF: Look, the fact is, all the things we want to do, they only work at a larger scale. You can't have autonomous cars that are only driving around three blocks. We can't afford to create a supply chain for tall timber, build a factory, just to have it make six buildings. The numbers don't work.

VERNER: You know, when we say we can't promise more land, we're not just being dicks for the sake of being dicks.

LASHER: Debatable.

VERNER: We don't own the land you want. Quayside is the parcel we own. That's it.

DAVIS: And even suggesting to you that we could somehow promise more land, it breaks a ton of procurement rules.

DOCTOROFF: I mean, I think we all know that there are rules and there are rules.

VERNER: What the hell does that m—

DOCTOROFF: And the thing is, we want to break ground as soon as possible.

FLEISSIG: What do you mean, you want to break ground?

LASHER: And now we arrive at the purpose of this meeting. We've decided we want to be the developer.

DAVIS: I beg your pardon?

DOCTOROFF: We've been working on it, and it's clear that the real estate play here could help our bottom line. If we can show a profit in terms of the real estate, it can offset any expenses we'll be taking on the innovation front. Especially given that data sales are off the table as a source of revenue.

DAVIS: You can't. There's no pathway for you to become lead developer in our agreement.

DOCTOROFF: Our current agreement. That's why we're here working on the next agreement. But even so, even as a developer, our investment only makes sense for us if we can also have at least a hundred more acres. Will's been briefed on all this.

A beat.

FLEISSIG: Look. Sidewalk Labs should get Quayside right from an innovation standpoint, let's do that part right, and then we can discuss a path forward on another parcel. Once everyone sees what we've built at Quayside, once everyone's excited, everything becomes possible.

VERNER: But there's no way around it: any more land, you'll have to go into competition for it, get all the approvals, bring the City around.

DAVIS: But as for being the Quayside developer, it's just not possible, not right now, given the public's reaction to—

DOCTOROFF: No. Fuck that.

FLEISSIG: Sorry?

DOCTOROFF: Fuck that! When we got here, it was yes yes yes, then it was I dunno, maybe, and now it's fucking no after fucking no.

FLEISSIG: Look, Dan—

DOCTOROFF: *(slamming his hand on the table)* No! You look! Fuck that! Fuck this!

DOCTOROFF *storms out. A pause.*

DAVIS: You know, we've all read his book.

VERNER: We know this is a thing he does.

LASHER: The book. Dammit. Okay. Let's, I dunno, take a break, regroup in fifteen?

FLEISSIG: Sure. Okay.

The lawyer shuts their folder, sits motionless. The others start to rise, shuffle papers, take out phones.

The word [INTERMISSION] *begins slowly fading up, as do house lights.*

Suddenly, DOCTOROFF *pokes his head back in.*

DOCTOROFF: Did it work?

The house light goes back down, [INTERMISSION] *snaps out.*

LASHER: Everyone's read the book.

DOCTOROFF: Dammit. I need a new move. Okay.

DOCTOROFF *returns to the table.*

Look, let's get the new agreement signed. We can work from there.

FLEISSIG: I, yes, okay.

DOCTOROFF: You don't have to put anything in it about more land. You don't have to make any commitments in writing.

FLEISSIG: Okay.

DOCTOROFF: As long as you understand where we're at. We have to figure out how to make this viable. We have to turn a profit.

FLEISSIG: No, sure.

Lights begin to fade and [INTERMISSION] *fades up.*

LASHER: And we have to show a path to profitability sooner rather than later. Who knows how long it will take to exploit internationally whatever patents we file as a result of whatever we create here.

VERNER: Understood. But so you know: the procurement process through the City for more land can be as long as five years.

DOCTOROFF: Yeah, but c'mon.

DAVIS: No. There's no "c'mon." There's no getting around those rules.

LASHER: I feel like, if we can just get in front of the right people, maybe we can—

VERNER: Look, can we focus on Quayside? You guys really need to focus on Quayside.

Lights are out. In the dark:

DOCTOROFF: No sure, but, you know: c'mon!

End of Act One.

During intermission Will FLEISSIG *enters and sits at the boardroom table. He tries several seats. At some point, a grey individual arrives and sits at the seat apart from the table, the seat that contained the lawyer in the last scene. The individual does not acknowledge* FLEISSIG. *The lights go down.*

ACT TWO
SCENE ONE

[Still fiction.]

{July 3 or 4, 2018.}

Lights up. Helen BURSTYN *enters.*

BURSTYN: Will.

FLEISSIG: Helen.

BURSTYN: Am I late? Were you waiting long?

FLEISSIG: Possible I got the time wrong.

BURSTYN: I see.

She sits. FLEISSIG *glances at the individual.*

Will, I've asked you here today to discuss something serious.

FLEISSIG: *(fake terrified)* Uh oh.
Ha ha.

BURSTYN: *(she was taking out a folder)* Sorry?

FLEISSIG: No, nothing. Who's that?

BURSTYN: Ah. That's Francis Bacon. Francis is from a consultancy the board has retained.

FLEISSIG: Sorry, your name is Francis Bacon?

No response.

BURSTYN: We've asked Francis Bacon's firm to do a three-sixty review on your performance. As CEO of Waterfront Toronto.

FLEISSIG: Ah. Okay. Listen—

FLEISSIG's phone rings.

(checking and declining the call) Sorry. This is Dan. Sorry. Okay. I thought something was up. Staff getting pulled from meetings to be interviewed for some mysterious thing. Okay. I think I know what the report will contain, Helen. I admit I'm a big-picture guy and I've struggled with detail. But we're finally completing the Plan Development Agreement, and now Sidewalk can begin the work on the master plan. I want to propose that—

BURSTYN takes a page from the folder, slides it across the table.

BURSTYN: This is a letter of resignation. If you're okay with the wording, we'd like you to sign it.

A pause.

FLEISSIG: Now hang on—

BURSTYN: This, obviously, comes from the full board.

FLEISSIG: Details. I mean, I get it, details aren't my strong suit, and okay, I was unprepared for some meetings, and yes, I did fail to brief the board in a timely manner. Sometimes. But, I mean, really? This?

BURSTYN: It's much more concerning. You once sent Dan Doctoroff to brief us instead of coming yourself. It was a complete waste of our time.

FLEISSIG: I was going to attend along with him. I got held up—

BURSTYN: We're concerned that the company you brought us, that it's a problematic company, and that your relationship with that company is somewhat porous.

FLEISSIG: The company *I* brought—

His phone rings again.

Sorry. It's Dan again. I thought I turned it off. Helen—

BURSTYN: We understand that management has to develop a relationship with a vendor, but as you've been working alongside them, we feel your inconsistency—your messiness—may have extended into the realm of . . . promise-making. Possibly.

FLEISSIG: I haven't— Look. You know how this is. Keeping someone on the hook, keeping them involved, sometimes, yes, okay, you over-promise if necessary, off the record, on small things, and then you manage expectations later.

BURSTYN: Will—

FLEISSIG: We're looking for a COO. The board approved the search for a COO. For someone to manage the details day-to-day. That will really help me. Structure will help me. We could have that person in place by the end of the month.

A pause.

Listen. Okay. You don't want to do this. The process is at a very delicate moment, all the controversy, we're all trying to manage, and yes,

Sidewalk has proven to be a tricky partner here, but listen: this project will fail. If you remove me from the centre of this, it will fall apart.

BURSTYN: We believe we can handle it.

FLEISSIG: I'm not being—that's not ego talking—I'm trying to say—

A different phone rings.

BURSTYN: Will, please.

FLEISSIG: *(digging out an Android phone)* Ugh, this is, it's a phone Dan gave me. So he can always reach me. This is what I'm dealing with. This is what I'm saying.

BURSTYN: Will, it's clear that—

FLEISSIG: No! Listen!

A beat.

Forget Sidewalk. Forget Dan. We are doing something extraordinarily hard. We are working out what this will be, in public, with the public's input, and only our goal of sustainable housing in a completely new way as the thing to hold onto. People can't handle the ambiguity, the messiness of figuring it out, and so they're filling in the project with their own fears. That's what's happening. Don't let that dictate these decisions. If the press, if anyone senses we aren't united right now—

BURSTYN: You know, if you had done a better job of managing our image in the press, if someone—

FLEISSIG: YOU WOULDN'T LET US TALK TO THE PRESS.

A pause.

I— I— God.

BURSTYN: Will?

FLEISSIG: I just got my kids into school.

She waits.

Please. I'll quit the minute there's a hole in the ground.

BURSTYN: No.

FLEISSIG: No?

BURSTYN: We can't wait for things to improve. We have to do something, it has to be big, and we have to do it fast.

FLEISSIG: This is your recommendation, *Francis Bacon*?

BURSTYN: It's the board's decision.

A pause.

FLEISSIG: I'll stay until there's an interim CEO in place?

BURSTYN: Michael Nobrega has agreed to step in temporarily.

[The Waterfront Toronto org chart appears with the board at the top, management below. Fleissig is crossed out from the CEO position and Nobrega is copied and pasted from the board position and inserted at CEO.]

FLEISSIG: Jesus.

BURSTYN: *(nudges the letter)* Will, please.

At a loss, FLEISSIG *reads the resignation letter. A beat.* BURSTYN*'s phone pings and she looks at it.*

Ah.

FLEISSIG: There's a typo.

BURSTYN: Sorry?

FLEISSIG: *(takes out a pen)* You spelled "contribution" wrong.

BACON *looks at his copy of the letter.*

BURSTYN: Sorry. Listen. This is Michael Nobrega. He has a suggestion he wants to float.

FLEISSIG: Okay.

BURSTYN: He wonders if, post-resignation, you'd agree to stay on as a consultant?

FLEISSIG: What?

BURSTYN: Your knowledge of the project is obviously invaluable.

FLEISSIG: Post-firing.

BURSTYN: Yes.

A beat.

It's a delicate moment for the project, as you've said. Any continuity you can offer after vacating the job would be incredibly helpful.

A beat.

This thing really could go off the rails. That would be a lot of hard work down the drain.

A pause.

FLEISSIG: Okay.

BURSTYN: Okay?

FLEISSIG: It's too important. Okay.

BURSTYN: Will, really: thank you.

SCENE TWO

TREE emerges. They were hiding somewhere, or perhaps was disguised as BACON.

TREE: Honestly, I find it hard to believe too, but the guy got fired and then agreed to hang around and help out.

Hi, welcome back. I'm still a tree, don't worry about it. Let me explain why he got fired, after being CEO of Waterfront Toronto for three years and starting the two biggest projects in the agency's history, ostensibly for the sin of being disorganized.

During the following CAM enters the boardroom and sets up for a meeting. He runs through the slides in a deck, arranges chairs. Eventually, DAVIS and VERNER join him and bring pencils, notepads, water, and a birthday cake.

The Plan Development Agreement between Sidewalk Labs and Waterfront Toronto, which detailed how they were going to work together, was supposed to take six weeks to complete. It took eight months. During that period, Sidewalk was constrained from describing what it had in mind for the project, and Waterfront largely didn't talk to the press because it didn't want their relationship with Sidewalk to seem like a foregone conclusion when they were still negotiating with the company. And into that vacuum rushed a lot of negative press. A LOT.

[*Globe and Mail*, March 2, 2018.]

VOICE 1: The high didn't last long. In the months since the announcement of Sidewalk Toronto, skeptics have been pouring buckets of cold water on the idea. Some fear that Sidewalk Lab's parent, Alphabet, is out to filch all of our personal data. Others suspect it of scheming to take over the Port Lands, the huge, barely developed stretch of real estate on the east side of the harbour.

[*The Guardian*, October 24, 2017.]

VOICE 2: Why settle for tax breaks or coding camps when you can lay claim to an entire neighbourhood? The city itself is turned into just another platform on which Silicon Valley can build and test new technologies while extracting value.

[Bianca Wylie, *Medium*, February 23, 2018.]

VOICE 3: Months of relative silence from both Waterfront Toronto and Sidewalk Labs has done nothing good for the work. Torontonians, and people around the world, have poured their hopes, concerns, demands, and suggestions into the quiet.

[*Washington Post*, August 8, 2018.]

VOICE 4: . . . so far, the virtual world has been something we opt into, and can opt out of if we so choose. It's one thing to willingly install Alexa in your home. It's another when publicly owned infrastructure—streets, bridges, parks, and plazas—*is* Alexa.

[Bianca Wylie, *Huffington Post*, May 9, 2018.]

VOICE 3: We need a hard discussion about data, surveillance, and infrastructure. But we aren't getting much more than urban-planning platitudes and jargon . . . nothing about the project is clear.

[*Toronto Star*, March 5, 2018.]

VOICE 4: Tech companies are carving out portions of cities as their own kind of sovereign territories.

[*Globe and Mail*, October 5, 2018.]

VOICE 1: What happens with Toronto's waterfront infrastructure will have profound and permanent impacts on the digital rights and prosperity of all Canadians because IP and data—our century's most valuable extractive resources—spread seamlessly. Any data collected can be reprocessed and analyzed in new ways in the future that are unanticipated at the time of collection and this has major implications for our privacy, prosperity, freedom, and democracy.

TREE: Some of the arguments were thoughtful, some were hyperbolic, some were disingenuous, and some were unhinged. You can decide which is which. This tree's only point is that the volume of this criticism, the tide of it, rose during that eight-month period and then it continued to rise. Here's a tiny example of how this chorus created its own momentum. Remember when Eric Schmidt said way back in Act One when we were all young and innocent:

SCHMIDT: Our founders, years ago, got really excited at the idea of taking all the technical things that we know and applying them to cities. They kept talking about all of the things we could do if someone would just give us a city and put us in charge. Mmm, that's not how it works, guys! For all sorts of really good reasons!

TREE: It was a deprecating joke about how dumb the founders of Google were when they started thinking about how to tech up a city.

And the reporting on the day described the quote as a joke. Here's the *New York Times*:

[*New York Times*, October 18, 2017.]

VOICE 4: " . . . and our founders got really excited. We started talking about all of these things that we could do if someone would just give us a city and put us in charge."

That is, of course, an outlandish idea. "For all sorts of good reasons, by the way, it doesn't work that way," Mr. Schmidt acknowledged.

TREE: But soon enough, the quote got stripped of the joke context and was used to build arguments about how scary Google is:

[*The Atlantic*, February 13, 2018.]

VOICE 1: Sidewalk Labs is the realization of Google's long-standing dream to, as the former Alphabet executive chairman Eric Schmidt once put it, "give us a city and put us in charge."

[*The Intercept*, November 13, 2018.]

VOICE 2: The genesis of the thinking for Sidewalk Labs came from Google's founders getting excited thinking of "all the things you could do if someone would just give us a city and put us in charge."

[*The Times of London*, October 20, 2017.]

VOICE 3: Larry Page, Sergey Brin, and Eric Schmidt liked to talk about "all of these things that we could do if someone would just give us a city and put us in charge."

[*Up Magazine*, November 4, 2019.]

VOICE 4: Sidewalk Labs grew out of Google's founders' enthusiasm for the idea of bringing innovation to the world. "Everything we could do if someone gave us a city and put us in charge of it."

[*Globe and Mail*, October 8, 2018.]

VOICE 1: The most insightful comment came when Eric Schmidt, Google's former executive chair, said they had realized their long-running dream for "someone to give us a city and put us in charge."

TREE: That quote is a little example of how the controversy fed on itself, instead of on fact, to grow. Waterfront Toronto had its hands full managing its partner Sidewalk Labs; it had no idea how to deal with the mounting bad press.

So that's the pressure the Waterfront board was under when it decided to fire its CEO. And when things start breaking against you, they often continue to break against you. In fact, the momentum of things breaking against you tends to build and—

VERNER: Yes, yes, we get it! Thank you! Jesus Effing Christ!

TREE: Sorry, sorry. I'll leaf. Hey, here comes Matthew Pegg.

SCENE THREE

The boardroom, where preparations for the meeting are complete. Chief of Toronto Fire Services Matthew PEGG *appears at the door.*

PEGG: Hey ho.

DAVIS: Chief Pegg.

VERNER: Chief Pegg, come in.

PEGG: Hi, guys.

VERNER: Kristina Verner.

PEGG: Hey, Kristina.

DAVIS: Chief Pegg. I'm Meg Davis.

PEGG: I met your dad.

DAVIS: Really. And this is Cam Malagaam from Sidewalk Labs. Cam, Matthew Pegg, Chief of Toronto Fire Services.

CAM: Great to meet you in person, sir.

PEGG: *(of the cake)* Just in time for the party, I see.

VERNER: Yes! Well, a little birdie told us it was your birthday.

PEGG: This is for me?

DAVIS: Absolutely.

PEGG: Hey, guys, thank you so much!

VERNER & DAVIS: Of course! Our pleasure!

PEGG: Not my birthday though.

DAVIS: What?

PEGG: Nope. Birthday's in January.

VERNER: Goddammit. But—

CAM: This is the first time someone's gotten bad info off of the Internet.

A beat.

VERNER: Well, there's no law that says we can't enjoy it anyway. Will you take a slice?

PEGG: For sure! Thanks!

VERNER: Great! Okay . . .

VERNER *looks for a knife. There is no knife. Through the following, she considers her options, then gives up. Later in the scene, when he has more and more time to himself, Matthew* PEGG *will gaze sadly at the cake.*

DAVIS: Honestly, that's about par for the course around here lately.

PEGG: Yeah, you guys have been up against it. I've seen the papers.

DAVIS: We spend all our time putting out fires, if you know what I mean.

A beat.

PEGG: My wife said that the hardest part about becoming fire chief was going to be listening to everybody's fire puns. But it turns out it's actually the fires. Anyways! What can I do ya for?

DAVIS: Now that we've got an agreement with Sidewalk Labs, we're focusing on some of the details of the development. We want to look ahead and try to anticipate where the snags will occur in terms of bylaws, zoning, that kind of thing. So today is a preliminary look at some questions we hope you can help us with when it comes to the City.

CAM: There's two topics we wanted to speak to you about today. I've prepared a little slide deck, but much of it will be familiar because it was all in the document I sent you last week.

PEGG: Oh yeah. I didn't look at that.

CAM: Okay! No problem. So one project is a little pilot we want to run outside the building here on the street, right on Queens Quay Boulevard. We want to tear up the street and the sidewalk.

PEGG: They'll love that at the City.

CAM: Ha ha, yeah.

PEGG: Who's paying for that?

CAM: Oh, we will. A hundred percent of the cost.

PEGG: That'll help. And why?

CAM: So here's the thing. I love pavement. I think about it all the time.

VERNER: He's not kidding.

CAM: Streets are part of the public realm, they're something we all share. So, but, how can we make them better for people? A street has a narrow sidewalk relegated to the side of the road, then a curb, then a vast expanse for cars. What we want to test is: what happens if we remove the sidewalk, take out the curb, put it all on the same level, and replace the pavement with these:

He indicates the pavers that are part of the set.

These are the hexagonal pavers we're thinking of using through parts of Quayside. They'll be heated to melt ice and snow—that way it's safe for bikes and pedestrians—and they're modular so that if there's a pothole you don't have to tear up the street to fix it, just take out the paver.

PEGG: And this is all on the same level? The street and the sidewalk?

CAM: Correct.

PEGG: And what keeps the cars from running over the people who have wandered onto the road without realizing it?

CAM: The pavers have lights, and the lights delineate where cars go and where people go.

PEGG: Lights.

CAM: Yes. Car path is indicated by one colour, people paths by other colours.

PEGG: I mean, you're aware Toronto drivers are terrible.

CAM: Um . . .

PEGG: Just down the road here, we built a right-of-way for the LRT to go underground. It's in the middle of the road, bright flashing lights all around it telling cars not to go in it. Cars regularly get wedged in there, and we have to pull them out.

[https://www.thestar.com/news/gta/2017/10/18/car-stuck-in-queens-quay-tunnel-again-despite-do-not-enter-signage.html.]

CAM: I get it. There will still be separation between pedestrians and the road. Trees and furniture. But this way, we can change the road's use more easily. Limit cars to one lane or no lanes if we want to use the road for a street party or a farmer's market. We can eliminate parking if traffic is heavy, again, using the lights, and let people park if there's little traffic.

VERNER's phone pings. DAVIS's phone pings. They take a look.

PEGG: I see. Okay, I guess that sounds—

DAVIS: Oh boy.

{July 30, 2018.}

CAM: What's up?

DAVIS: No, nothing, carry on.

PEGG: And you want to do this out front here?

CAM: Yup. Just this block. We want to demonstrate some of our ideas so that the public can give us—

VERNER: *(to DAVIS)* Deliberately timed to fuck us.

PEGG: Hey now!

VERNER: Sorry. It's just—a Waterfront Toronto board member just resigned.

[The Waterfront Toronto org chart appears. Board members populate it and then Julie Di Lorenzo is crossed off.]

DAVIS: It's fine.

CAM: Over Quayside?

DAVIS: Yes. She had reservations about the project from the outset.

VERNER: We are finally completing the Plan Development Agreement, it's taken months. We're announcing it tomorrow. She's effectively ruining the first piece of good news we've had in a year.

PEGG: That's rough.

CAM: Maybe she'll resign quietly?

DAVIS: Unlikely.

Julie DI LORENZO *pops out.*

DI LORENZO: I do not believe it was the intention of the three levels of government to allow a single company to become our filter, our gatekeeper, and our agent. Yet through an unconventional series of circumstances, I feel we have allowed this to happen.

VERNER: Fuck a biscuit. Should we, I dunno, prepare some kind of response or something?

DAVIS: It looks like the board is putting out a statement thanking her for all her hard work.

VERNER: Is that enough?

DAVIS: I think so. Who knows. Sorry, guys. Cam, please continue.

CAM: Okay. So, obviously we're going to need to tear up the street, install the electrics, and then the pavers.

PEGG: How long?

CAM: We think the road will be down to one lane for a week or so, with limited pedestrian access.

PEGG: That means three weeks. And shut down completely for how long?

CAM: We think closed overnight for three nights, closed completely for one day. Does that seem realistic?

PEGG: I guess? Maybe?

DOCTOROFF *appears in the door.*

DOCTOROFF: Hey! Cam.

CAM: Hey, Dan.

DOCTOROFF: I was looking for you, guy. Hey, Meg. Hey, Kristina.

DAVIS: Dan.

DOCTOROFF: Hi, I'm Dan Doctoroff, CEO of Sidewalk Labs.

CAM: Dan, this is Matthew Pegg, chief of Toronto Fire Services.

PEGG: How's it going?

DOCTOROFF: Hey, I was going to get in touch with you. You guys discussing tall timber?

CAM: Not yet. Right now we're talking about the street pilot.

DOCTOROFF: Great. Hey, listen, I just found out that Alphabet bought a company that's working on flying autonomous vehicles. So make sure that there's space out there on the paver pilot to land a flying car.

DAVIS: Seriously?

VERNER: Seriously?

CAM: Seriously?

DOCTOROFF: One hundred percent seriously.

DAVIS's phone pings. VERNER's phone pings.

Cam, did you pick up the centrepieces yet?

CAM: I was going to pick them up in the morning.

DOCTOROFF: Because we need one more. We're doing one more table.

VERNER: *(off her phone)* What the ever-loving fuck?

DAVIS: It's fine.

VERNER: No, it's not! In what way is this "fine"?

DOCTOROFF: What's up?

{October 2018.}

VERNER: Our offices are being raided.

DAVIS: It's not a raid.

VERNER: What would you call it?

CAM: What's going on?

DAVIS: Okay, so the Auditor General of Ontario has been conducting a value for money audit of Waterfront Toronto. It's been happening for weeks, and obviously we've been co-operating fully.

VERNER: And right now there are two guys from the AG's office standing in our offices and demanding that we hand over computers and passwords.

DOCTOROFF: Uh-huh.

DAVIS: I don't understand this. All we've done is co-operate.

DOCTOROFF: It's politically motivated. This is how you generate some bad press if you need to.

A beat.

Would be my guess. My advice is: don't give them anything.

DAVIS: But who's behind this?

CAM: You guys have a new premier, right?

[https://globalnews.ca/news/4260716/doug-ford-pcs-win-majority-government/.]

DAVIS: There's no way.

VERNER: Except it's happening. What do we do?

DOCTOROFF: Someone's trying to gin up controversy in advance of that report coming out.

DAVIS: *(off her phone)* Okay, okay. It looks like there's a couple of board members there, and they're standing firm. They're basically shaming the guys into leaving empty-handed.

CAM: Wow.

DOCTOROFF: Some guys show up to do a raid, and they get shamed into leaving? Canada's adorable.

PEGG: Hi, guys. Uh, should I go?

VERNER: No no no no no. Sorry.

DAVIS: Sorry, Chief Pegg.

PEGG: You sure? Things seem kind of busy.

VERNER: Absolutely, it's all fine now. Where were we?

PEGG: No idea.

CAM: Just nailing down that you're okay, in theory, with the street pilot project so that we can approach the City.

PEGG: If you get a yes out of the City, you've got a yes out of me.

CAM: That's— Okay! We'll take it.

DOCTOROFF: Chief Clegg, I want you to email me personally if you have any questions about this stuff, any concerns at all. Or talk to Waterfront, of course. These guys are great!

DAVIS: Thanks, Dan.

PEGG: For sure. You know, I shook hands with her dad when I was a little boy. It was on the front page of the *Star*.

DOCTOROFF: No kidding. Who was your dad?

DAVIS: My dad was Bill Davis. Premier of Ontario from 1971 to 1985.

DOCTOROFF: No way! Fantastic.

PEGG: Great guy. Transformed the province.

CAM: His motto was: bland works.

DOCTOROFF: Really! I get that as the motto.

CAM: He stopped an expressway here in Toronto. Just like Jane Jacobs did.

VERNER: He saved the downtown.

[https://www.tvo.org/article/the-streets-belong-to-the-people-why-a-premier-killed-the-spadina-expressway.]

DOCTOROFF: No way! That's something to be proud of.

CAM: Of course, he also killed a waterfront housing project too. It was called Harbour City.

[https://www.blogto.com/city/2010/09/remembering_harbour_city_torontos_unbuilt_town_on_the_lake/.]

DAVIS: You've absorbed a lot of our history, haven't you, Cam?

CAM: For sure!

VERNER's phone pings.

PEGG: Toronto is really, really good at killing projects. It's like our superpower.

VERNER: Dan?

DOCTOROFF: Yes!

VERNER: Are you hosting a lunch for a hundred "thought leaders" tomorrow? Without us?

DOCTOROFF: Yes!

{October 17, 2018.}

VERNER: Fucking *why*?

DOCTOROFF: We need to get people on board. We need the—sorry to say it—elites on board with the project.

VERNER: We just fucking agreed—sorry, Chief, one sec—we just agreed that we would speak with one voice on Quayside. That Sidewalk acting on its own would be unacceptable.

DOCTOROFF: It's lunch! No one said anything about lunch. Chief, great to meet you.

(to CAM*)* Come see me when you're done here, okay? I'm worried the centrepieces aren't opulent enough.

CAM: Okay.

DOCTOROFF goes.

VERNER: Fucking hell.

DAVIS: Okay. Well. Nothing we can do about it today. Let's keep this moving. Chief, thanks for sticking with us. Cam, what else do we need to cover today?

CAM: Well, Chief, we need your support on mass-timber buildings. You know anything about them?

PEGG: I know that they're building one right down the street here.

CAM: Yes. It's for George Brown College.

PEGG: I guess the feeling is, when it goes up in flames, we just lose a bunch of kids, no big deal.

CAM: Oh boy.

PEGG: That was a joke.

VERNER's phone pings. DAVIS's phone pings.

CAM: Oh! Okay. So actually, mass timber has a higher fire rating than concrete.

PEGG: Oh yeah, no no, mass timber's great.

DAVIS: Are you seeing this?

{July 25, 2018.}

VERNER: Goddamn it.

DAVIS: The DSAP hasn't even done anything yet.

VERNER: God fucking dammit.

CAM: Guys?

DAVIS: Sorry, Cam. Sorry, Chief.

VERNER: John Ruffolo just resigned from the DSAP.

PEGG: What's a DSAP?

[The Waterfront Toronto org chart pops up. DSAP appears below and to the right of staff. It populates with names. As soon as John Ruffolo's name fills in, it gets crossed out.]

DAVIS: It's our Digital Strategy Advisory Panel. Experts who are helping us get the digital privacy and data-use piece of Quayside right.

VERNER: He just joined! The panel hasn't even met yet.

DAVIS: He doesn't like the non-disclosure agreement we asked him to sign.

RUFFOLO appears.

RUFFOLO: I am still unclear what exactly the nature of the confidential matters might be, and I cannot sign such a vague and broad agreement as I do not even know exactly what I am agreeing to.

DAVIS: We're still working on the parameters of the NDA.

VERNER: This seems fishy.

DAVIS: Nonetheless, we—

Their phones ping again.

Son of a—

VERNER: *(simultaneously)* Son of a *bitch*.

{October 4, 2018.}

CAM & PEGG: What?

VERNER: Now Saadia Muzaffar has quit the DSAP.

[Muzaffar is crossed off the DSAP.]

PEGG: What's her deal?

MUZAFFAR pops on.

MUZAFFAR: In the last eleven months, Waterfront Toronto's utter lack of leadership regarding shaky public trust has been astounding. There's a growing list of squandered opportunities to take charge of the narrative that would clarify the boundaries of who's in charge.

DAVIS: And she didn't like Sidewalk's job posting for local architects.

MUZAFFAR: Sidewalk Labs is asking potential local consultants to hand over any intellectual property that is developed to the Alphabet-owned company.

{Late August 2018.}

VERNER: *(at CAM)* That was the fucking stupidest thing you guys could have done, issuing a call for architects without us and saying all their work would be owned FOREVER by Sidewalk Labs.

CAM: I know. I know. That was New York.

VERNER: We're trying to convince people that the things that get created at Quayside, that value will stay in Canada.

CAM: No, I know. It's just how they're used to doing things.

DAVIS: Cam, it's well past time for your bosses to acquire a degree of sensitivity as to how *we* do things.

PEGG: Guys, I'm just gonna—

CAM, DAVIS, & VERNER: Sit down!

PEGG: Yup.

VERNER: You guys have got to stop fucking us.

CAM: Couldn't agree more.

DAVIS: Okay. Okay. We need two new panel members.

Three phones ping.

{October 15, 2018.}

Sidewalk Labs has released their data-management proposal for Quayside.

VERNER: *(scrolling)* And it is . . . not good.

CAM: No. I know. New York again.

DAVIS: This is very . . . hand-wavy. Very unspecific.

CAM: Yeah.

VERNER: There's the data trust . . .

CAM: *(to* PEGG*)* A data trust is where all the data collected at Quayside is held securely by a third party.

PEGG: Okay.

CAM: There would be rules around who gets access to the data, and for what.

PEGG: Wicked.

VERNER: And none of those rules are articulated in this document. Jesus.

More pings.

{October 16, 2018.}

(off the phone) FOR FUCK'S SAKE.

DAVIS: Three members of our data panel have threatened to resign based on how lousy this document is.

[The org chart appears again, and asterisks pop up beside DSAP members Andrew Clement, Pamela Robinson, and Teresa Scassa.]

CAM's *phone pings.*

CAM: Okay, Ann Cavoukian has resigned.

VERNER: I'm going crazy. Right here, right now. Fucking ballfuck fucknuts, right here.

PEGG: Who's Ann Cavoukian? Can I have cake?

CAM: Former Privacy Commissioner of Ontario. We hired her to consult for Sidewalk Labs on data privacy. I guess she didn't like the data-management proposal either.

DAVIS: Okay, we need to fill seats on the DSAP with experts, we need to craft a response to this document, we need to—

Pings.

(under her breath) Fuck around.

{December 7, 2018.}

VERNER: *(now she's laughing)* Doug Ford has fired the three provincial appointees to our board.

[The Waterfront org chart. The board populates with the provincial appointees crossed out.]

DAVIS: Including our board chair.

VERNER: His timing is impeccafucking fuck. Jesus.

DAVIS: Okay. Okay. So first we have to—

Pings.

VERNER: WHAT NOW, BITCHES.

{December 8, 2018.}

DAVIS: The Auditor General's report is out.

Silence as all three scroll and read. For quite a while.

TREE *enters with a little knife. Through the following, they cut a little snick of cake.* PEGG *watches closely. When* TREE *goes,* TREE *takes the knife.*

TREE: The Auditor General of Ontario is an agency that evaluates how well or how poorly public money is being spent. It conducts dozens of audits per year, across all the departments the government controls. This value-for-money audit of Waterfront Toronto was unique in a couple of ways. First, this was only the third time in the AG office's hundred-and-fifty-year history that it conducted an audit of an arm's-length agency like Waterfront Toronto. Second, the money being spent wasn't Ontario taxpayers', but Sidewalk Labs'. But when you're in the newspaper as much as this project is, well, that's what happens.

VERNER: *(still reading)* This is . . . this is . . .

DAVIS: Incredibly bad.

TREE: *(as they exit, mouth stuffed)* Oh god, so is this cake! I love it!

CAM: How much coverage does an Auditor General's report usually get?

DAVIS: Not much. Usually.

VERNER: But in this case.

CAM: Uh-huh.

VERNER: What do we do? We can't just say thanks for this. This has to be responded to. There are so many things here that are inaccurate. She's clearly been influenced by the negative press.

DAVIS: If we respond with anything other than "thanks very much," they'll just keep coming after us. We have to let it—

A ping.

Ah. And now you and I have been called to testify before the Access to Information, Privacy and Ethics Committee of parliament. Federal parliament. To answer for the Auditor General's report.

A pause.

VERNER: We're done. We don't come back from this.

DAVIS: I mean . . .

VERNER: No. That's it. The water's over our heads.

PEGG: Guys. This is good for you.

They all look at him.

This is a provincial report, right? The Auditor General is the province?

VERNER: Uh-huh.

PEGG: You're being offered a national stage to make your case.

A beat.

DAVIS: He's right.

VERNER: What are you talking about? They're going to kick us around the block. On fucking TV.

DAVIS: Listen, if we stop now, the project is dead. And maybe it is dead, and this is pointless, but don't you want the chance to finally describe what we had in mind? Put it on the record?

VERNER: Ugh. Fine. Can I blame you?

DAVIS: Absolutely.

They're going. CAM*'s phone pings.*

CAM: Oh shit. Dan's been called to testify before that committee too.

DAVIS: Dan's on his own.

CAM *goes.* PEGG *gazes sadly at the cake.*

SCENE FOUR

{February 21, 2019.}

VERNER and DAVIS arrive at the committee hearing. A gavel bangs.

THE CHAIR: Welcome to this sitting of the federal Access to Information, Privacy and Ethics Committee, order please. Today we have with us from Waterfront Toronto Meg Davis, Chief Development Officer, and Kristina Verner, Vice President of Strategic Policy and Innovation. We will hear questions for these witnesses from Peter Kent, Conservative MP for Thornhill.

KENT: Ms. Davis, Ms. Verner, thank you for being here. Ms. Davis, a pleasure to see you, I knew your dad.

DAVIS: So did I.

KENT: Pardon?

DAVIS: Nothing, I'm a bit nervous.

KENT: Okay. I have some questions raised by the Ontario Auditor General's report and Waterfront Toronto's relationship with Sidewalk Labs. Waterfront put out an RFP to develop the Quayside site in March 2017, and Sidewalk Labs was chosen. Immediately there were whispers that the political fix was in on this project, that Prime Minister Trudeau wanted Sidewalk Labs, a Google company, to win the bid and build a data-driven, so-called smart city. The prime minister himself admitted as much during the opening event for the development, mentioning that he and Eric Schmidt had been discussing the project for some time, after which Schmidt stated how thrilled he was that Canada was, quote, "giving him a city."

Since then, the AG asserts, the board of Waterfront Toronto has revealed it had a shorter-than-usual timeline to approve the development, and there has been a resignation over the project at the board. There have been several resignations at the data panel, as well as worldwide criticisms of the project because some believe it has the potential to be the worst digital privacy invasion in history.

And now a leading Canadian tech entrepreneur has written an editorial in the *Globe and Mail*—he's a very rich man and so clearly knows his stuff—saying, and I quote: "Canadians will be treated to glitzy images of pseudo-tech dystopia while a foreign company profits from the IP and data that Canadian taxpayers fund and create." He says, "Sidewalk Toronto is a colonizing experiment in surveillance capitalism. Of all the misguided innovation strategies Canada has launched over the past three decades, this purported smart city is not only the dumbest but also the most dangerous."

He looks up, expectant.

DAVIS: Was that a question?

KENT: Well, I guess, what do you think of all that?

DAVIS: Mr. Kent, let me try to address your concerns in order.

Did the prime minister rig the selection: The process was overseen by former Ontario integrity commissioner Justice Coulter Osborne. He approved our choice of Sidewalk Labs. It was also overseen by a steering committee independent of Waterfront Toronto. They approved our selection. We had evaluations done by external subject-matter experts, including KPMG and the Canadian Urban Institute, and independent legal opinions provided by Dentons and McCarthy Tétrault. Each of *them* agreed with our selection of Sidewalk Labs as preferred proponent. Can you explain if it's likely, or possible, for all of these external, independent, and trustworthy actors to conspire to do the prime minister's bidding?

KENT: Well—

DAVIS: And keep it a secret?

KENT stays silent.

Sir, my question wasn't rhetorical.

KENT: No, it does not seem likely, Ms. Davis.

DAVIS: Thank you. The selection process was the second longest in our history, at 159 days, so no, the process was not rushed. The AG chose to focus on the second stage of the process, which she correctly notes was six weeks long, and ignored, for some reason, the four-month stage that came before it.

KENT: Are you saying the Ontario Auditor General is wrong?

DAVIS: In this, yes.

KENT: That's a troubling assertion. How did she make this mistake? She's an extremely careful public servant.

DAVIS: I don't know.

Opinions about the process being rushed appeared online, and were picked up in various places, including by the tech entrepreneur you quoted earlier. Whom I note the AG chose to interview even though he has no first-hand knowledge of the situation—he's not a stakeholder nor in any way connected with the project. At any rate, it's possible the Auditor General was influenced by something she read or was told. But it's untrue. It *is* true that the board was required to vote on our selection of Sidewalk Labs four days earlier than planned, to accommodate the schedules of the VIPs who attended the project launch.

KENT: Ah, I see! So—

DAVIS: But it's also true that the board had six separate information meetings about the selection in the weeks prior to the final decision being announced. They had ample time to consider every aspect of the decision they were asked to make.

KENT: So it's your contention that, in spite of everything we've read about the Quayside project, everything we've heard from a variety of experts, there's no problem at all with this deal? Everything is above board?

DAVIS: There is no deal. We have invited Sidewalk Labs to offer us solutions. We challenged them to offer us ways to build more efficiently and make a climate-friendly neighbourhood. Until we choose the ideas we like and sign off on a master plan, a draft of which they haven't given us yet, we have no obligation to them.

KENT: The documents leaked this week from the master plan indicate that Sidewalk Labs has designs on more than the twelve acres of Quayside. It expects to be involved in the development of the entire Port Lands.

DAVIS: In the RFP we invited proponents to think of solutions that might not be feasible for a twelve-acre site, but could become doable over a larger area. A cooling system that uses deep lake water might be too expensive to consider for just four or five buildings at Quayside but could work financially across a larger district. But again, there's nothing that obliges us to take what Sidewalk Labs is proposing. And as for them looking beyond our twelve acres, Waterfront Toronto doesn't own anything beyond the Quayside site. Sidewalk can't obtain from us what we don't own.

KENT: It's pretty clear a lot of people think Waterfront Toronto is getting steamrolled by this high-powered tech company.

DAVIS: The master plan, when Sidewalk Labs presents it to us, will be subjected to a rigorous internal review by Waterfront Toronto. This will be followed by reviews at all three levels of government to which Waterfront Toronto answers. It will also receive a high degree of public scrutiny. We have structured the process to ensure that we can't be steamrolled.

KENT: Fair enough. But this is a new kind of neighbourhood, loaded with sensors collecting all kinds of data all day, every day. And isn't it true that Sidewalk Labs could take the data generated at Quayside and sell it to whomever they like?

VERNER & DAVIS: It's not true.

KENT: There's a lot of people who worry that's exactly what will happen.

VERNER: I know. That worry has been aired so often over the last few months it's now taken as fact. But it's not true. Our very first agreement with Sidewalk Labs stated that the data collected at Quayside cannot be sold. We're well aware of Google's reputation, and so we've made sure they understood from the outset that the sale of data to a third party is, and will always be, prohibited.

KENT: I see. Now, we're told Canada lags on the data front, that this government's laws around data are hopelessly out of date. I'm told Barcelona has a stringent set of laws on privacy and data use. What do you think of Barcelona's data regime?

VERNER: Barcelona is excellent.

KENT: Would you be okay with Barcelona being imposed here?

VERNER: Barcelona is excellent for Barcelona.

I know there's real anxiety about this element too, about data and privacy, and a desire for an immediate, straightforward solution. But we can't just slot in Barcelona and call it a day. Quayside will be unique and will require rules of its own.

To that end, we've been developing our own principles for data use and security at Quayside.

The principles are: compliance with existing law; data minimization so that the least amount of data is collected; no third-party sharing; Privacy By Design embedded in any proposed technology; comprehensive security architecture; a commitment that the data collected will be stored in Canada; and accountability, real accountability, in the collection, use, and storage of data. Any ideas offered by Sidewalk Labs will have to conform to that governance model.

KENT: Can't Sidewalk agree to your principles then change the terms of service or whatever at some point in the future to use the data however they want?

VERNER: They won't be able to, legally. But they might try. Or a third party working on Sidewalk's platform at Quayside might try. The City or the province might even decide to try. Digital infrastructure has to be maintained, just like roads and bridges. Data governance will be an ongoing job.

KENT: Okay, but, fair, but . . . but you have to understand: the Cambridge Analytica scandal, the resignations, all the bad press you've had, the Ontario Auditor General's concerns, not to mention Google's reputation, it all points to an impending disaster. Wouldn't you agree, Ms. Verner, that where there's this much smoke there's fire?

VERNER: As someone who's devoted to data, I'd say that when there's this much smoke, there's something making a lot of smoke.

THE CHAIR: We'll have to hold it there, Mr. Kent. Thank you to our witnesses—

DAVIS: If I may, I just want to say . . . Sorry, may I make a statement?

THE CHAIR: Of course, Ms. Davis.

DAVIS: Waterfront Toronto has made mistakes. We just signed a Plan Development Agreement with Sidewalk. It supersedes the framework agreement we entered into when we chose Sidewalk Labs. And we grossly underestimated how complex the PDA would be, and how long it would take to reach this agreement—it's taken eight months. In the meantime, we, pointlessly, kept the original agreement secret. This gave everyone already disposed to anxiety about what we're up to reason to speculate, and to draw unfortunate conclusions. Waterfront had its reasons for this secrecy, but ultimately Waterfront was wrong. It was a mistake.

And I want to assure you all, that that will not be Waterfront's last mistake. Waterfront has deliberately put itself in an unusual position, one of uncertainty and open inquiry. We will be rigorous, we will be careful, but we need to remain uncertain because we're trying to make something new. And it will take a long time before we'll have our answers. In some ways, we won't know if we've succeeded until rents are set on those affordable units based on the hoped-for cost savings of construction. We won't know if we've been successful until we find out how close to zero those buildings' carbon emissions are. And once people are living at Quayside, of course we will continue to learn. The first time a UPS truck gets stuck trying to turn around in a loading bay, we will learn something. The first time an automated garbage-hauling machine fails, we will learn something. And we will eventually learn which of our choices didn't work, and which did, and, crucially, which choices can be refined and duplicated elsewhere. And of course, it won't really be a neighbourhood at all until people are living their lives there. Until they're buying groceries, or until a kid takes a swimming lesson. There's a long road before we get to that point, and the question is: Can we all live with a degree of uncertainty, of not knowing, while we work this out?

A beat.

THE CHAIR: Thank you, Ms. Davis. Ms. Verner, do you have anything you want to add? Do you want to make a concluding statement?

VERNER: Yes. Meg Davis is the absolute tits.

THE CHAIR: Okay. Let the record reflect. Thanks for your time.

DAVIS and VERNER gather their things.

Up next will be Dan Doctoroff, CEO of Sidewalk Labs—

DOCTOROFF: *(pops on)* Hi, guys!

THE CHAIR: But first—hi, Mr. Doctoroff—first the committee will take a short recess.

DOCTOROFF: Ah! Okay!

He disappears.

SCENE FIVE

DAVIS and VERNER return to the office. Josh O'KANE is waiting in the boardroom. The cake abides.

[Josh O'Kane, tech reporter for the *Globe and Mail*.]

[An arrow points at O'Kane.]

O'KANE: Hi, guys! Do you want to hear a joke I'm working on?

VERNER: Hi, Josh.

DAVIS: Josh. What can we do for you?

O'KANE: Can I ask a couple of questions? On Quayside?

{February 14, 2019.}

VERNER: Why does the *Globe and Mail* always send their tech reporter to ask about our housing development? Why not send the sustainability reporter, or the architecture critic?

O'KANE: That's a really good point. I'm going to bring that up. Hey how many architects does it take to screw in a light bulb?

VERNER: I don't know, how many?

O'KANE: Well, what's your budget?

A beat.

DAVIS: Yes, I see.

O'KANE: No good? Okay, what do you call it when you kill your mother by sleeping on top of her? Matricide.

DAVIS: You had a question?

O'KANE: *(digging in his bag)* Right. So you guys must be feeling like the worst is behind you, no one's quit in over a month.

VERNER: Yes, we do feel back on track.

DAVIS: And now we wait to see what's in the MIDP.

O'KANE: Yeah, the MIDP. You know, I really don't think "Master Innovation and Development Plan" is an improvement on the phrase "master plan."

(of the cake) Someone's birthday?

DAVIS: No, it's—that's from before. Anyway, to answer your questions: yes, we do feel like we've found our feet after a rocky few months. The search for a new CEO continues, and meanwhile we have nothing but confidence in Michael Nobrega to lead us. Sidewalk continues to work on proposals to make Quayside the unparalleled development we know it can be. We have seen bits of the MIDP, but not the whole thing, and we won't comment on it until we do. But we're on track, we're optimistic, and we're excited for the future.

O'KANE: Got it. Okay. Were you aware that Dan Doctoroff made a presentation to the Alphabet brass back in November about Quayside?

[Doctoroff pops on screen. Through the following it populates with Alphabet execs in their small squares. Doctoroff exists in his larger square, sometimes disappearing and replaced with a slide from his deck.]

DOCTOROFF: Hello, Mountain View!

DAVIS: Not aware, but we assume he's in regular contact with his parent company.

O'KANE: His presentation included details about Quayside, the eastern waterfront, and their plans for how they intend to profit from this project.

VERNER: We were unaware of this and we didn't participate in that meeting.

DAVIS: It wouldn't be appropriate for us to comment.

DOCTOROFF: Hey, guys! Hoping to get started in just a sec.

O'KANE: Understood. I have screenshots of the slide deck he used for this presentation. I want to show them to you and get your comments.

DAVIS: Okay.

> *He hands them several pages each, stapled horizontally. They begin to read.*

O'KANE: As you can see . . .

DAVIS: Hang on?

DOCTOROFF: Okay, let's get started.

VERNER: *(under her breath)* Fuuuuuuuu.

DOCTOROFF: Hi, everyone. I'm happy to give everyone at Alphabet a sense of where we are at with the project in Toronto, what the timelines are like, and what the potentialities are, especially in the area of revenue streams over the medium- and long-term for Alphabet.

O'KANE: The deck makes it look like Sidewalk has fully developed and costed plans well beyond Quayside—

DAVIS: Hang on.

[The Quayside site pops up in Doctoroff's deck.]

DOCTOROFF: First, the Quayside parcel. As you can see, it's narrow and backs onto a raised expressway. The site is twelve acres. Not huge. The potential here is for approximately three million square feet of retail, mixed housing, and light industry, as well as public realm. But, while Quayside is a limited opportunity for us, it represents the first step in a much larger project. Quayside, as they say, is key.

VERNER: He did this when?

O'KANE: Last November. I just obtained these slides a few days ago. You're saying you had no idea—

VERNER: Can you— Can you give us a bit of time with this? When's your deadline?

DOCTOROFF: Here's the eastern waterfront of Toronto.

O'KANE: I'll need a comment from you by four o'clock.

[The eastern waterfront.]

DOCTOROFF: The entire eastern waterfront is almost five hundred acres, about the size of Chelsea in Manhattan. It has the scale to make possible a truly innovative, cutting-edge district of the future.

O'KANE: I also need a commitment from you both you won't share these images or make copies of them.

VERNER: Sure. Okay.

O'KANE: Meg?

MEG is looking at the floor.

VERNER: She promises too. We'll be in touch.

O'KANE goes.

DOCTOROFF: Polson Quay, Keating, Port Lands East and South, and this man-made island, known as Villiers Island.

VERNER: Meg?

No response.

DOCTOROFF: Almost all of it post-industrial brownfield, and most of it city-owned. The eastern waterfront will give us the scale we need to make a safe, sustainable community on the last vacant waterfront property in North America. And Alphabet would be first in line not only to benefit directly from this new model, but also to export its features around the world. The value for Alphabet will be ongoing, considerable, and at minimal risk. Canadian public institutions, hungry for the innovations we uniquely can provide, will assume most of the downside exposure.

As DOCTOROFF's presentation proceeds, the following happens: DAVIS begins to breathe heavily. VERNER watches her carefully. Still staring at the floor, DAVIS lifts her balled fists to the sky, slowly. They shake there. She lifts her eyes to the heavens. She shows VERNER her balled fists, helplessly. She rubs her balled fists in her hair, her eyes, her face. Down her body. If DAVIS could unball her fists, she would probably tear off her clothes. She encounters a button on her cardigan. She pulls the button off, throws it into the audience. She pulls off all the buttons, one by one. She pulls off the last button and, staring levelly at VERNER, *puts in her mouth. She chews, still staring at* VERNER. *She spits out the pieces.* DAVIS *makes sounds.*

DAVIS *goes to the table, takes a pencil from the cup, breaks it in half. She stabs the birthday cake with it. She repeats this with all the pencils. When out of pencils, she flips the cake over onto the table and, with her hands on the plate, methodically grinds and smears the cake and pencil bits into the table. When this is done, she removes her shoe and begins banging the plate with it, trying to break it. Finally,* VERNER *intervenes, gently taking* DAVIS*'s shoe from her.* VERNER *leads* DAVIS *off.*

Let me quickly outline the upside for Alphabet, and as I do, keep in mind that I won't today be including the value accruing to Alphabet from the patents we will hold on the innovations we will generate here. There's simply no way to know what that value is, so let's today focus on the real-estate and development potential.

Sidewalk will be named innovation manager for the entirety of the eastern waterfront, spurring the creation of the world's most innovative urban district by providing a MIDP and taking responsibility for the initial phase of vertical development at Quayside and Villiers West. We will create a financing package that will facilitate the development of horizontal infrastructure at Quayside, Villiers Island, and Polson Quay.

Mass transit, for example, which is currently non-existent in the district, will be financed through us. That will see returns based on incremental tax diversion. We and our partners will take from the city a slice of the difference between current property tax and the expected post-development, much higher property tax.

As innovation manager for the entirety of the eastern waterfront, Sidewalk will set design and innovation guidelines for vertical and horizontal development, including a radical rezoning of the entire area. While there is some current reticence on the part of the Toronto City bureaucracy for what we will require, Sidewalk has done an extraordinary amount of outreach to local, provincial, and federal politicians. We believe the obvious economic benefit our plan represents for the city and province will expedite regulatory hurdles.

So, as lead developer for part of the project, and innovation manager for the entire district, Sidewalk can expect to generate revenue in the following ways:

1) Proceeds from vertical development;

2) A share in uptick of land value on the entire geography for which Sidewalk is named innovation manager;

3) A share of developer charges and incremental tax revenue from all horizontal infrastructure we finance.

We estimate the value from these streams represents approximately six billion dollars to Alphabet over a thirty-year time period. And again, this figure does not represent the value of the digital value-adds which will accrue to Alphabet as proprietary developer.

Financing: Sidewalk is committed to being a careful steward of Alphabet's money. Our financial model includes potential partnerships with Canada Infrastructure Bank, McKinsey, and Goldman. Risk mitigation and capital-structure arbitrage will ensure that our capital remains functionally protected until returns are manifested.

What are the challenges? We are forging relationships in Canada among tech elites and the political class, and while there is a degree of code-switching incumbent on us as Americans, we are learning rapidly. In Canada, power is more diffuse, and we are learning that few people who possess power, even politicians, like to have that fact pointed out—a kind of photo-negative approach to ours in the US.

There has been some bad press, based primarily on Google's reputation on data acquisition and exploitation, some of it from a successful, high-profile Canadian tech entrepreneur. We believe that, as we roll out innovations in the Quayside development and across the eastern waterfront, we will prove ourselves as good stewards of the land, and as we work to change minds among skeptics, we will be seen as a net benefit to the city, and to the country . . .

The screen fades. DOCTOROFF*'s voice fades. After a beat of darkness, a French lesson begins.*

SCENE SIX

Mayor John TORY *sits at his desk.*

A VOICE: Je comprends l'art.

TORY: Je comprends l'art.

A VOICE: Cette sculpture n'est pas de l'art.

TORY: Cette sculpture n'est pas de l'art.

A VOICE: Ce sandwich est magnifique! Ce sandwich est de l'art.

TORY: Ce sandwich est magnifique! Ce sandwich est de l'art.

Steve DIAMOND *is at the door. Steve* DIAMOND *is low-key.*

A VOICE: Le boulanger est un véritable artiste.

DIAMOND: John?

TORY: Steve! Come in.

DIAMOND: Am I interrupting?

TORY: No no. Just trying to get in a little practice.

A VOICE: La plupart de l'art est dégoûtant et bourgeois.

TORY *stops Duolingo on his computer.*

TORY: What can I do for you, Steve? Take a seat.

{December 2018.}

DIAMOND: Thanks, Your Worship. I won't take up too much of your time. I just wanted to let you know, I'm going to step down from the Waterfront board.

[The Waterfront Toronto board chart appears, with its several vacancies. A line is drawn through Steve Diamond's name.]

TORY: Really? Everything okay?

DIAMOND: Everything's fine. I just, I'm tired. My term is almost up, and it seems like this is the moment to go, before the MIDP drops on us like an anvil.

TORY: Is it going to be a mess?

DIAMOND: From the bits we've seen, I think Sidewalk is more interested in doing the things they're interested in doing instead of helping us out with a few buildings and a park.

TORY: Jebus Christmas. This whole thing.

DIAMOND: Anyway, I think it's best if I depart now so whoever replaces me can have a chance to—

TORY: I can't let you go.

DIAMOND: What?

TORY: Steve, you're the only developer on the Waterfront board. You're the only one with practical knowledge, the expertise, to keep these negotiations on track. Sidewalk is like a drunk baby with a pistol. You have to keep this thing together.

[Diamond's name is un-crossed.]

DIAMOND: John, I appreciate all that. But I'm here telling you as a courtesy.

TORY: You can't go. In fact, Steve, you have to change the drunk baby's diaper for me. You have to take this thing over. You have to take charge.

DIAMOND: John—

TORY: I'm making you board chair. You're the only one remotely qualified to unfrig this friggin' thing. You don't have to stick around until people move into the buildings, but just get this thing back on track. You can quit when there's a hole in the ground. Steve. It's got to be you. What do you say?

[Steve Diamond moves to the board chair position.]

DIAMOND: Well. Do I have the authority to walk away from the table if Sidewalk won't meet our terms?

TORY: Absolutely. And look, if the deal dies, you'll be a hero to everyone who's hated this thing from the outset.

DIAMOND: Yeah.

TORY: But if you can bring Doctoroff to heel, then maybe we can still make this goshforsaken thing work.

DIAMOND: Well. Okay.

TREE appears.

TREE: Don't do it, Steve Diamond.

TORY: He said he's doing it.

TREE: Maybe this will change his mind.

TREE drops the boxed MIDP on TORY's desk.

The Master Innovation and Development Plan is ready.

{June 2019.}

TORY: Jebus Kripes!

TREE: The MIDP: 1,524 pages, four volumes, glossy, showy, sexy as hell. And with the exception of a couple of hundred pages, not in any way the thing you were asking for.

TREE hands out volumes. DIAMOND and TORY start leafing through.

How many mes were destroyed in the making of this opus?

[Pics from the MIDP of the IDEA District are projected.]

TORY: Holy crumbs. They want . . . 190 acres? Built across five sites? They want to be developer for all this?

DIAMOND: Looks like they want to be developer for two sites, and the uh, innovation partner, whatever that means, for the rest of it. They want . . . developer fees, fees for investing in infrastructure—

TORY: —fees for building our transit—

DIAMOND: —advisory fees, venture-fund fees. They want to build and own a mass-timber factory, fees for tech implementation, and whatever money they make selling the tech created here. And a performance fee at the end for doing a great job.

TORY: *(taking another volume)* Look at all this. It'll take weeks to sort through all this bullcarp.

DIAMOND: Yeah.

(quietly) Christ.

TORY: Steve, I'll understand if you don't want to take this on.

A beat.

DIAMOND: John, fuck that. I'll do it.

SCENE SEVEN

[The map of the IDEA District stays up.]

Boardroom. The cake-smeared table. VERNER *and* DAVIS *already in place.* DAVIS *still dishevelled.*

DIAMOND *joins. A beat of quiet, then* DOCTOROFF *and* LASHER *enter.*

DOCTOROFF: Guys! Sorry. Are we late?

Nothing from the others.

(as they settle) Hey, Steve. You know, I've been running around since dawn. How would you guys feel if we ordered in some lunch?

DIAMOND: This might not take that long.

DOCTOROFF: What are you—

DIAMOND: Dan, here's an open letter we have released to the community.

DAVIS *hands out pages.* LASHER *and* DOCTOROFF *read.*

DOCTOROFF: You sent this out?

DIAMOND: *(checking his watch)* Four minutes ago.

DOCTOROFF: You felt the need to let people know Waterfront had nothing to do with the creation of the MIDP?

DIAMOND: We did.

LASHER: "Whether the Quayside project proceeds or not, the conversation we are having is important for all of Toronto." Whether Quayside proceeds or not?

DIAMOND: Correct.

DOCTOROFF: Now look, Steve—

DIAMOND: Sidewalk Labs has been a chaotic and untrustworthy partner.

LASHER: Untrustworthy?

VERNER: We know, for example, you've been filing patents in the US based on things you've learned here.

LASHER: So?

VERNER: We're supposed to share intellectual property.

LASHER: In case you haven't noticed, we're up here spending fifty million dollars trying to figure out how to do the thing you're asking for.

VERNER: In case you haven't noticed, you've fucked this thing with both hands. Even the people who were on your side before the MIDP now think you're here to colonize us. A hundred and ninety acres!

LASHER: We don't want a hundred and ninety acres.

We want to be developer on two sites, that's it. Quayside and Villiers West.

DIAMOND: No.

LASHER: No?

DOCTOROFF: No?

A beat.

LASHER: Well, fuck me and fuck off then, I guess?

DOCTOROFF: Steve. This is the plan. This is it. If you're serious about trying to do the things you say you want to do, then this is it. There is no other way to scale the very expensive things you want unless we can spread the cost over the entire district. Sidewalk Labs wants to develop Quayside to control the innovation side, provide proof of concept. And Villiers West is the new Google headquarters. But the rest of this, it's us working with local developers, whoever you want, to build out the district according to the climate and affordability standards you set.

DIAMOND: Guys, we don't want to waste your time. You seem to have a radically different idea of what should happen here. It's not what we asked for, it's not what we want.

LASHER: Maybe the MIDP was a mistake, maybe it's too much, that's on me. I wanted to make a document people could get excited about.

DAVIS: It's not a document. It's a fifteen-hundred-page ad for your services aimed at markets other than the one in which you're currently working.

LASHER: That's, okay, that's fair. But look. Don't throw away the entire project because I made this mistake. We're here, we can be less chaotic, and this plan, this plan is achievable.

DAVIS: Even if this matched our vision for the district, we can't authorize this plan because we don't own the land. Which you know. Which you've always known.

LASHER: Yes, we understand that, but the city owns most of this land. If the City approves this plan, then this is the plan.

VERNER: It's incredible that you've spent this much time here and you still don't understand how any of this works. There's a process.

DIAMOND: No one in this room can give you the thing you're asking for.

DOCTOROFF: It's funny. I've tried for two years to figure out which room I should be in to get what I want. You know what? There is no room. There is no person or group of people I can persuade. Power here is so spread around, so diffuse, it's like people want to pretend it doesn't exist. Even the people who have power pretend they don't. I used to think that was cultural, that there's some kind of Canadian reticence that makes power invisible here. But it's not Canadianness. It's not politeness to a stupefying fault. It's because power kept out of sight is also kept out of mind. If the power isn't evident, then no one can get too upset when it's used. It's a frictionless way of getting your way. It's intentional. The political structures here ruthlessly serve the maintenance of the status quo.

So once again, let's do the little dance: I'm confident we have the mayor and a majority of city council on board with some version of this plan. And if the elected representatives of the citizens of Toronto are good with this, then tell me what the issue is?

DAVIS: The City is obliged to put all the land it wants to sell up for bids. By law. There's a procurement process developers follow. There are zoning and planning restrictions that your plan completely ignores.

DOCTOROFF: The City can do things a different way if it chooses to. It can cite a project as being in the economic interest of the region and give it to a developer without process. It's done it in the past. And Waterfront Toronto has, in the past, worked to change planning and zoning. Why are you acting like there is no path here? Jesus, even the transit, everyone freaks out over the idea of us running an incremental tax-financing scheme as if you've never heard of such a thing! They get used in Canada all the time. Stop acting like you're helpless. It's been two years of this shit!

DAVIS: You've created no good will with the people who are rightly suspicious of Google. And you've managed to make every level of government turtle on this.

VERNER: Do you know how bad this has to be for the prime minister, the original Google fanboy, to duck your calls? He is ducking your calls, right?

DAVIS: This project is so toxic no government will help us with it. Do you understand?

DOCTOROFF: Look, I don't mean to tell you your guys's jobs, but that's on you. We're here to offer innovations, and you guys are supposed to execute.

LASHER: We're here with a plan. Is it big? Yes. Is it scary? Maybe. But it's your job to sell it.

DOCTOROFF: The IDEA District can be a historic transformation. But you have to step up and take it. Meg, Kristina, this is the cusp of—

DIAMOND: Dan. Dan. Look at me. It's Quayside only. Go ahead and yell if you need to.

DOCTOROFF: FUCK YOU, STEVE.

> DOCTOROFF *gets to his feet. He paces for a beat or two.* VERNER *is going to say something, but* DIAMOND *indicates she should remain silent.*

Quayside only. And we're the developer?

DIAMOND: No. You can be co-developer with a Canadian partner.

DOCTOROFF: Fuck around.

A beat or two.

LASHER: Maybe this is more trouble than it's worth. Maybe we should start over in Buffalo or Detroit. At least we wouldn't have to put up with this bullshit.

DIAMOND: You could definitely start over somewhere else.

VERNER: Sure. What's the shelf life of a Google side bet that isn't producing any income? Four or five years?

DOCTOROFF: Okay: make it Quayside and Villiers West. Make it Quayside and Villiers West and I think we can make it work. Villiers West is the site of the Google headquarters, it's the anchor of a new tech district. We develop that too, with a Canadian partner if we must, and, okay. Quayside is twelve acres, Villiers West is another twenty, that's thirty-two acres, that keeps us in the game.

DIAMOND: That sounds good to me.

DOCTOROFF: Okay.

DIAMOND: We can't offer you that.

DOCTOROFF: WHY NOT?

DIAMOND & DOCTOROFF: There's a process.

DOCTOROFF: Kill me.

A beat.

LASHER: So, what. That's it?

Silence.

Unbelievable.

VERNER: Sorry.

LASHER: You're sorry. Do you know what would happen, the last two years, when I would tell people I was flying up to Toronto to work on this thing? How immediately bored they would become?

VERNER: I'm sorry people find you boring, you fucking dickless fuck.

DOCTOROFF: All right.

DAVIS: I have a thought.

VERNER: Hudson Yards looks like Las Vegas with the shits.

LASHER: Hey!

DAVIS: What if . . .

VERNER: And the High Line is fucking stupid!

DOCTOROFF: *(gasps)* Don't you *dare*!

DIAMOND: Okay, okay. Meg? Something?

DAVIS: What if . . . What if this: Villiers West is owned by an agency called PortsTO. Maybe we can do a land swap with them, give them a bit of the water's edge or the slip at Quayside in return for the Villiers West site.

DOCTOROFF: A swap gets around the process?

DAVIS: It could.

DIAMOND: That's a good idea. Sure. We can try that. See what they say.

DOCTOROFF: Okay, okay, okay. Good. How about that, we're back in it.

DIAMOND: Not so fast. What are you forgetting?

LASHER: The purchase price for Quayside.

DOCTOROFF: Yes. The purchase price for Quayside. Now—

DIAMOND: It's assessed at $590 million.

DOCTOROFF: Yes. And what discount are you offering?

DIAMOND: No discount. That's the price.

DOCTOROFF: No discount. What are you talking about, a developer gets a discount for adding value to the property.

DIAMOND: Yes. You don't.

DOCTOROFF: Fucking— May I enquire why we won't receive the same consideration as every other developer since the dawn of time?

DIAMOND: Well, you're on the record last November saying the profit to Alphabet on this Toronto conquest was going to be—what was the figure?

VERNER: Six billion.

DIAMOND: Six billion dollars. For the real estate alone. Under those circumstances, it would be unseemly for us to offer a discount on the purchase price of the land.

DOCTOROFF: You know I was bullshitting when I said that.

DIAMOND: I'm happy to keep that between us. A couple of other things. The MIDP has been so damaging that we're going to need to reset the relationship. We've drawn up a list of threshold issues—that it's Quayside only, that the price is the price, that the privacy and data provisions in the MIDP are dogshit and will be set by Waterfront and Waterfront alone. You'll have to agree to those threshold issues, very publicly, before we proceed. We need you to be a good partner. We will be a good partner to you. But we need to woodshed you first. Okay?

DOCTOROFF: Fine. Wouldn't be the first time.

And Villiers West? You think you can make that happen?

DAVIS: It's possible.

VERNER: It's possible it's possible.

DIAMOND: It's not impossible.

LASHER: Well I'm reassured.

DIAMOND: We will get back to you on Villiers West as soon as we know something. We want the Google campus to happen, Dan. We want all of this to happen. But on our terms.

DIAMOND stands. DAVIS and VERNER stand. TREE materializes.

TREE: And then they shook hands, and we all lived happily ever after.

I mean, obviously not. Soon after this, two things happened. When the bureaucrats at the City of Toronto got wind of the land-swap idea, they issued a letter. Here's the letter.

[The letter from the deputy city manager is displayed.]

You don't need to read the letter. It just reminds everyone that there's a process to be followed, which could take several years, and Sidewalk was welcome to bid on the Villiers West site along with everyone else. The letter is a kind of master stroke. The letter is—if you knew that a project was teetering on the brink of failure, and you wanted to nudge it over the edge, this is the letter you would write.

So the land swap was off the table. And the second thing that happened was this:

> {December 2019.}
>
> [The Alphabet org chart returns. Sergey Brin and Larry Page are removed and Sundar Pichai is installed as CEO.]

Brin and Page stepped down from running Alphabet. And how does the new CEO, Sundar Pichai, feel about Larry Page's side bets? He's not a fan.

PICHAI: There's a process of evaluation underway for the side-bet companies. They represent a drag on Alphabet's balance sheet that shareholders rightly find troubling.

TREE: All of which meant, well, this:

SCENE EIGHT

{May 6, 2020.}

VERNER and DAVIS in the Waterfront boardroom. DOCTOROFF appears on screen. He looks tired.

DOCTOROFF: Hey, guys.

DAVIS: Good morning, Dan. We wanted to discuss the dimensions of the smallest affordable-rental units, to make sure we're all comfortable with the size. They seem small to us. And though they are efficient, we wonder if—

DOCTOROFF: Guys. Sorry to interrupt. Sorry. Listen. Sidewalk Labs is pulling out now.

A beat.

We're stopping our operations there. We're done.

A pause.

Guys?

DAVIS: What?

DOCTOROFF: Yes. Look. I have a lot of experience with failure.

VERNER: What are you—

DOCTOROFF: A lot of experience. So, listen: it's only a failure if you let others define it as a failure.

DAVIS: Hang on.

DOCTOROFF: It's up to you to make the thing you want out of this thing others might call a failure. It doesn't have to be your word for what's happening.

DAVIS: Hang on. *Why?*

DOCTOROFF: There's no path for us. And our time's up. Look, I gotta go. I gotta go. Thanks, guys.

He disappears. A beat. CAM *runs on.*

CAM: Guys!

VERNER: What the— Oh man.

CAM: Guys! Hi! Hey, remember when I took Dan and the others to meet the members of the Mississaugas of the Credit, because they're the treaty holders for the Quayside land? Well, I didn't want to say anything then but, I can tell you guys now—

DAVIS: Cam. What are you doing here?

CAM: So Sidewalk has reached an agreement with the Mississaugas of the Credit to offer them ten percent of the units at Quayside in an equity partnership.

DAVIS: What?

CAM: Yes, a path to ownership on 144 units. We're committing to making space for them, real space, at Quayside. You know, according to the calls to action from your Truth and Reconciliation Commiss—

DAVIS: Cam. CAM. Check your email.

CAM: What?

CAM looks at his phone. DAVIS looks down.

Well.

I used to go to bed at night praying you wouldn't notice we were clowns until there was a hole in the ground.

We had unserious leadership—we were a fucking mess—yes. We were clowns. But we came here not knowing that NIMBYism is a way of life here. It's bigger than ice hockey. You might have warned us.

I think you guys may have actually invented a whole new kind of NIMBYism. So . . . there's one innovation I guess.

I guess the question is: Why are we fucking around like this? Why? Hundreds of thousands of people are coming to live here in the next few years. And in the next eight years the climate tips into something hellish. These two crises, housing and climate, this project was a step, a small step, towards addressing these crises. The kind of thing we should have been taking up a generation ago. So yes, late, and yes, clowns, but it would have been a start? Our thing wouldn't have fixed anything, but it would have been a step?

You're scared of the data harvest, fine. You're scared of getting screwed on the money, fine. You don't like a private company taking a portion of tax revenue, fine. But the moment has long passed when you can tell this kind of project to fuck off and then pat yourselves on the back and call it a day. Say no to us. But just saying no is no longer an option. Like: if not this, then fucking what? What?

VERNER comes to CAM, holds his hand.

Dozens of people I work with are fucked. They quit jobs in tech and planning and design and whatever because they believed this was worth doing and that's fine. That's sad but that's fine, that's life, but, like, if not this gigantic dumb idea, then what?

What do we do? I mean—

> *VERNER hugs CAM.*

Yeah. Okay.

> *He goes. VERNER watches him. She notices DAVIS, who is still looking down. DAVIS makes a fist. Is DAVIS going to go off again? A pause. Then the fist unballs.*

> *DAVIS looks up.*

DAVIS: Do you have the list of companies we spoke with prior to issuing the RFP?

VERNER: What?

DAVIS: The people we spoke with for the RFI.

VERNER: I . . . yes. Why?

DAVIS: *(sitting, opening her laptop)* We need to build the next RFP. I'd like to start now.

VERNER: . . . Okay.

> *VERNER searches her phone for a document, finds it, sends it. DAVIS's laptop pings softly.*

DAVIS: Thank you.

VERNER, after a beat, joins DAVIS at the table, opens her laptop, and starts working. Lights dim.

We read:

[In the months after it left Toronto, Sidewalk Labs shed all of its senior management. Dan Doctoroff resigned as CEO in December 2021. The viable parts of Sidewalk Labs were folded into other Alphabet companies.]

[Cam Malagaam is an amalgam of the thirty or so young urban designers, engineers, and architects that worked at the Toronto Sidewalk Labs office at 307 Lake Shore Boulevard East.]

[A picture of the Norway maple at 134 Yorkminster Road.]

[The Norway maple at 134 Yorkminster Road abides.]

[In 2018, the Ontario government cut the size of Toronto city council in half. Fewer elected officials serving greater numbers of people means council is even more reliant than ever on Toronto City staff to develop and execute policy.]

[Josh O'Kane's nickname, One in a Million, refers to the proportion of jokes he tells to the ones his friends actually like. He currently writes for the *Globe and Mail* Arts section.]

[In 2022, the Ontario government conferred on John Tory special powers under the strong mayor statute. He promised he wouldn't use those powers. Unless he had to. He resigned in early 2023 rather than face questions about an extramarital affair.]

[Kristina Verner and Meg Davis still work at Waterfront Toronto.]

Lights fade on VERNER *and* DAVIS.

[Video of the empty, windswept Quayside site, with the caption: Live shot of the Quayside site.]

Blackout.

End.

ACKNOWLEDGEMENTS

In the summer of 2022, Chris Abraham called with a yet-to-be-published book and an idea for a speedy adaptation. He wanted to capture the timeliness of Josh O'Kane's narrative and he proposed a ridiculous schedule—eleven months to first day of rehearsals. This project has been the most fun I've had as a playwright in a long time, and Chris's bravery in programming a play that didn't yet exist is the first thing to be acknowledged.

Josh O'Kane was extremely generous with his time. He also realized quickly how a play would necessarily diverge from his careful reporting. He seems okay with that.

My thanks to Ari Cohen and Hannah Anderson, who loaned me their extremely comfortable house in Picton, Ontario, to write a first draft of the show.

My thanks also to the actors who read drafts of the script: Rick Roberts, Brenda Robins, Evan Buliung, Nancy Palk, Gregory Prest, Cam Laurie, and Mikaela Davis.

Michael Healey trained as an actor at Toronto Metropolitan University in the mid-eighties. He began writing for the stage in the early nineties and his first play, a solo one-act called *Kicked*, was produced at the Toronto Fringe Festival in 1996. He subsequently toured the play across Canada and internationally, winning the Dora Mavor Moore Award for best new play. *The Drawer Boy*, his first full-length play, premiered in Toronto in 1999, winning the Dora Award for best new play, the Chalmers Canadian Playwriting Award, and the Governor General's Literary Award (Canada's highest literary honour). It has been translated into multiple languages and continues to be produced regularly across North America and internationally. Healey's other works include *The Road to Hell* (co-authored with Kate Lynch), *Plan B*, *Rune Arlidge*, *The Innocent Eye Test*, *The Nuttalls*, *Are You Okay*, and *1979*. His trilogy focusing on Canadian values and politics—*Generous*, *Courageous*, and *Proud*—met with great critical success and have had multiple productions. In all, his plays have won the Dora Mavor Moore Award for best new play five times. He has also adapted works by Chekhov, Molnar, Hecht and MacArthur, Dürrenmatt, and Shaw for the Stratford Festival, the Shaw Festival, and Soulpepper. He continues to find work as an actor occasionally.